STANDARD-BASED SCORING vs GRADING: A CLASSROOM GUIDE

Danelle Elder

STANDARD BASED CLASSROOM GUIDE SERIES:

BOOK 2

Library of Congress Number

Copyright ©2015 by Danelle Elder. All rights reserved. No part of this publication may be reproduced or transmitted in any form or by any means, electronic or mechanical, including photocopying, recording, or any information storage and retrieval system, without permission from Danelle Elder, except when the pages of the Templates Appendix. Those pages (109-116), permission may be photocopied for classroom use. No part of these pages may be sold by any person or organization.

ISBN-13: 978-1517222789

ISBN-10: 1517222788

This book is printed by Amazon.com.

Editor: Diana D Elder

Contact and consulting information:

Email: danielleelder5702@comcast.net

CONTENTS

List of Figures 5

List of Templates 8

About the Author 9

Preface 10

    What is the Purpose of This Book

Acknowledgements 15

Introduction... 16

CHAPTER 1:

What is Standard Based Grading 18

    What is Standard-Based Teaching or Instruction

    The Nine Elements of Standards-Based Teaching

CHAPTER 2:

Target and Rubric Construction 23

    Rubric Construction

    Rubric Types.

    The Four Levels of a Rubric

CHAPTER 3:

Problems With The Tradition Mean System of Grading 36

    The Mean System of Grading Assessments

CHAPTER 4:

Standard Based Scoring 51

    Unit Alignment Guide

CHAPTER 5:

The Clear Problem with the Traditional Mean System of Grading 61

CHAPTER 6:

The Significance of 1% of Learning.. 66

CHAPTER 7:

Standard-Based Grade Organization....................................... 77

    Assigning a Grade Value to Standard-Based Scoring

    Flexible Standard-Based Grading Scale

    Amended Flexible Standard-Based Grading Scale

    Electronic Gradebook Scale

CHAPTER 8:

Determining the Grading Scale Percentage for Grade Assignment 87

CHAPTER 9:

What Holds Teachers Back From Accepting the Standard-Based Teaching Model.. 96

    Behavior vs Academic Reporting

    Behavior Reporting

    Teacher Consistently

The Last Word.. 107

Template Appendix... 108

LIST of FIGURES

Figure 1	Example of an Improperly Constructed Rubric	26
Figure 2	Another Non-Example of Rubric Construction	27
Figure 3	Rubric Levels of Learning	28
Figure 4	Correct Example of Rubric	30
Figure 5	Revised Bloom's Taxonomy	33
Figure 6	Taxonomy Selection Template	35
Figure 7	Assessment Outcome	38
Figure 8	Math Assessment Scoring Example	39
Figure 9	Surface Area Assessment Using the Mean System	40
Figure 10	Surface Area Rubric	43
Figure 11	Surface Area Assessment Using Standard-Based Teaching Method	44
Figure 12	Example Language Arts Rubric	47
Figure 13	Punctuation Assessment Using Standard-Based Method	48
Figure 14	Music Performance Rubric	49
Figure 15	Surface Area Rubric	52
Figure 16	Student Example of Surface Area Assessment	53
Figure 17	Punctuation Rubric	55
Figure 18	Student Example of Punctuation Assessment	56
Figure 19	Music Performance Rubric	57
Figure 20	Student Example of Music Performance Assessment	58
Figure 21	Unit Alignment Guide	59
Figure 22	United States Department of Education System of Grading	62

LIST OF FIGURES (CONT.)

Figure 23	Traditional Grading System - Standard-Based vs Grading System	64
Figure 24	Pie Chart of the Traditional Grading System Distribution	67
Figure 25	Pie Chart of a Child's First Walking Experiences	68
Figure 26	Pie Chart Showing 1% Determination of a Grade	69
Figure 27	Pie Chart Using a Scoring Rubric	70
Figure 28	People's Republic of China Map Assessment	71
Figure 29	Incorrect Construction of Math Assessment	73
Figure 30	Pie Chart for Example Science Assessment	74
Figure 31	Example of Level 3 Assessment for Plant Growth	75
Figure 32	Organization of Gradebook by Rubric Levels	79
Figure 33	Traditional System of Organizing Gradebook	80
Figure 34	Formative Assessments Used as Summative Assessments	81
Figure 35	Using A Flexible Standard-Based Grading Scale	83
Figure 36	Example Standard-Based Gradebook	84
Figure 37	Amended Flexible Standard-Based Grading Scale	85
Figure 38	Using Scoring Trends for Grade Determination	88
Figure 39	Comparing Trends to Percentages	88
Figure 40	Pie Chart with Rubric Content Breakdown	89
Figure 41	A Breakdown to Construct a Grade Percentage	90
Figure 42	Professional Development Using a Grading Scale Template	91
Figure 43	Grade Distribution Over Time, Nationwide	93

LIST OF FIGURES (CONT.)

Figure 44	Electronic Gradebook Example	94
Figure 45	Behavior Rubric and Report Card	100
Figure 46	Behavior Report Card Using Numbers	102
Figure 47	Behavior Report Card Using Faces	103
Figure 48	Behavior Report Card Using Letters	104

LIST OF TEMPLATES

Revised Blooms Taxonomy by Anderson and Krathwohl (2001)	**109**
Taxonomy Selection Template	**110**
Rubric Construction Template	**111**
Professional Development Using a Grading Scale Template	**112**
Unit Alignment Guide Template	**113**
Behavior Report card Using Numbers Template	**114**
Behavior Report card Using Faces Template	**115**
Behavior Report card Using Letters Template	**116**

ABOUT THE AUTHOR

Danelle Elder is a teacher in Spokane Schools, Spokane Washington. She has taught science and math in middle school and high school for almost 30 years.

She has three degrees from Eastern Washington University: B. A. of Education, B. S. in Geology and an M. S. Interdisciplinary Geology and Education degree.

She has also taught at Whitworth University in Spokane, Washington.

She was a precious metal geologist and a uranium geologist before she became a teacher.

She has published three books in the **STANDARD-BASED CASSROOM GUIDE SERIES:**

- **Standard-Based Teaching: A Classroom Guide**
- **Standard-Based Scoring vs Grading: A Classroom Guide**
- **Standard-Based Journaling: A Classroom Guide**

PREFACE

Some history...

Across the nation, endless focus has been given to creating standard-based report cards. Numerous books have been published about this topic. Expert after expert site each other adding nuances to the same goal: how to create a standard-based report card.

From this focus, Tomlinson and McTighe (2006) clearly define six principles of standard-based grading. These six grading guidelines will be mentioned later in the book. I feel these authors are the building blocks of standard-based grading. These guidelines require teachers to focus on learning standards and not behavior.

For the first, time teachers are directed to stop grading on the mean system. **Changing grading practices from the traditional percentage system (A = 90%, B = 80%, C = 70%, D = 60%) to a rubric supported scale is the goal of this book.** Dividing student learning into a four steps using a scoring rubric is an essential part of standard- based instruction.

Before I wrote my first book, **Standard-Based Teaching: A Classroom Guide**, I was frustrated because even after multiple committee meetings, reading books from experts and numerous articles with endless hours of discussion, my district was still missing what I felt was the key ingredient to standard-based instruction in the classroom. I had been to workshops with Ken O'Connor and Rick Stiggins. While informative, the missing ingredient was never mentioned by them either. The missing piece to standard based instruction, I felt, was the organizational framework the teacher needs in the classroom. The framework that allows teachers to align vocabulary, assignments, study guides, journaling, and assessments to a standard

I developed a system to support the use of a standard-based report card where level 3 is the state target. However, because I was a teacher and not a 'published expert', no proposal I made mattered... So, I published my first book, **Standard-Based Teaching: A Classroom Guide.**

Standard-Based Teaching: A Classroom Guide shows every step of this organizational system for classroom instruction for any content area. I tried to use examples from as many content areas as I could. This organizational system works for science, math, social studies, music, art and other content areas.

Standard-Based Teaching: A Classroom Guide instructs teachers about proper rubric construction, standard construction, as well as how to scaffold assessments and advanced learning. It also discusses briefly how to use a journal in a standard-based world.

This method of scaffolding learning components, from basic to complex, creates organization for all classroom activities. It clarifies to students and teachers exactly what gaps exist in student learning and what knowledge has been mastered.

For struggling students, special education students and English Second Language students, a proper scaffold rubric allows students to identify areas of weakness. Differentiating instruction using this method is a powerful instructional tool to use in today's classroom.

Often struggling students are easily overwhelmed. Failing test scores only reinforces what they believe about themselves... that they cannot learn; they cannot be successful.

Assessments that are differentiated from simple to complex concepts allow this struggling student to pass usually the first and second levels much more easily. This allows the student and teacher time to concentrate efforts on the more complex learning target. When students see themselves regularly passing the simpler levels of learning, they begin to see themselves in a positive way, as a learner.

One of the most gratifying experiences in my career has been influencing the change from a negative to a positive learning attitude in a child.

My state test scores rose significantly using this system. My special education and ESL subgroup scores rose, as those students classroom successes rose using this system. Also, **this system of organization allows teachers to sift through data and determine why students are not learning.** Since scores are layered by complexity of content, it is easy to see that a student who regularly fails the vocabulary assessments (level 1) also fails every scaffold level following that vocabulary test. **It is easy for the teacher to assess, at a glance, which students are struggling and what levels need more focused effort.**

I can easily assess if an **ESL student** is acquiring vocabulary or other concepts. The very same is true for **special education students**. I don't simply use a singular value; I use four **stratified values** to evaluate student learning.

This type of scaffolding and organized learning also helps to challenge students who need to be challenged beyond target learning. Teaching the **advanced level** (level 4) allows all students to be exposed to concepts beyond the target learning.

Since the publication of **Standard-Based Teaching: A Classroom Guide**, teachers have emailed me with questions about the scoring of papers and how to turn that scores into grades. When talking to teachers, it is clear that teachers are mixing the mean system with standard-based teaching. Without professional instruction which focuses on developing scoring rubrics and grading scales to create a grade, mixing the old percentage system with rubric scoring is a natural default for teachers. The outcome, however, is simply a muddled-up version of the traditional mean system of scoring and grading.

It is important to remember that **scoring rubrics and grading scales are not the same thing**. Grade reporting scales have been the focus of many publications and school districts. It is the scoring rubric that is missing in educational literature and all the supporting organization of all related activities surrounding this rubric. It is the scoring rubric that now needs to be the major focus in classrooms, as well as, how those scores determine a grade. **It is for this reason that I wrote Standard-Based Scoring vs Grading: A Classroom Guide.**

WHAT IS THE PURPOSE OF THIS BOOK?

Standard-Based Scoring vs Grading: A Classroom Guide will show teachers exactly how to create a scoring rubric. It will also show the teacher how to develop a system to change scores into a grades.

This publication will contrast the traditional mean system scoring with standard-based scoring. It will show how to calculate a grade for both grading without an electronic grading program, as well as grading with a grading program. It will also clearly define a scoring rubric versus a standards-based grading scale. It will give examples of student work showing scaffolding according to a scoring rubric.

In this book, I have tried to show examples from a variety of content areas. **This organizational system will work with any content.**

Like the first book in the series, at the end there are templates that the teacher may freely duplicate and use in the classroom to create proper rubrics and grades. The templates and instructional strategies in **Standard-Based Scoring vs Grading: A Classroom Guide** are compatible with the learning scales required in **Becoming a Reflective Teacher (Marzano, 2012)**.

The last book to complete the **Standard Based Classroom Guide Series**, is the **Standard-Based Journaling: A Classroom Guide** which gives teachers a thorough look at how a student should journal using a standard-based organizational system. Templates will also be included in this publication.

References:

Elder, Danelle (2012): *Standard Based Teaching: A Classroom Guide.* http://www.amazon.com/Danelle-Elder-Standard-Based-Teaching/dp/B00N4FR7R2

Marzano, R. J. (2012). *Becoming a Reflective Teacher*, marzanoresearch.com/classroomstrategies

Tomlinson, C. A., and McTighe, J. (2006). Integrating Differentiated Instruction and Understanding by Design. Alexandria, VA: ASCD.

ACKNOWLEDGMENTS

I'm approaching my thirtieth year of teaching. Not taking a typing class really came back to haunt me when writing this series. There is really nothing glamourous about writing a book when you do not know how to type.

Later my mother bought me a speech recognition software program. It has really made my life easier inside and outside the classroom. I'd recommend it to any teacher.

My mother has pushed me to continue publishing. After publishing the first book, **Standard-Based Teaching: A Classroom Guide,** I wondered what I might write about. But after watching other teachers struggle on their own and after receiving emails from teachers across the country, I realized there was more about the organization system I had created that could be put into print.

Fortunately my mother**, Diana Elder**, is the finest wordsmith I know. She is my backbone for publishing and spent a great deal of time reading and editing my writing. The teachers in her life did a great job teaching her writing and reading skills. I hope we are still producing the same highly skilled wordsmiths as we did in her day. The world needs good wordsmiths. Without her expertise and her encouragement, I seriously doubt that I would have begun my writing career.

I would also, like to thank my family, who spent endless evenings listening to me ramble on, (now that I'm not typing but speaking the contents of these books).

INTRODUCTION

Today, teachers are under an enormous amount of pressure the moment they step into their classrooms. Teachers are expected to collect data, evaluate their own teaching, address learning gaps in students and be scrutinized by administrators using complicated evaluation systems. Above all, teachers are expected to be a content expert that inspires students to learn.

> **Teachers are under an enormous amount of pressure.**

In addition to these pressures, teachers have been asked to evaluate and change their own grading systems. Often districts and schools are heavily involved in this change. The focus for grade change has mainly been developing a standard-based report card. Educational experts like Guskey and Bailey (2010), O'Connor (2009), and Stiggins (2006) are some of the many educational leaders that encourage schools and districts to abandon the traditional mean system of grading and implement standard-based reporting.

Changing to standard-based grading creates an increase in student academic performance (O'Connor, 2009). When there is a single learning target, teachers and students can clearly concentrate on the importance of the learning target. Teachers can cull any concepts that are not central to the target. This allows teachers and students to evaluate more easily what has been learned and what needs still to be learned. No time is wasted on distractions.

Many debates in districts and schools have centered on the grading scale percentages as it relates to a report card. Much scrutiny has been given to what these grades and percentages mean to parents. But virtually no time has been allotted to creating scoring rubrics for grade formulation.

Exactly how does a teacher create a grade using assessments?
Without professional development, an excess of interpretations by individual teachers has arisen regarding grade creation.

> Exactly how does a teacher create a grade using assessments?

Because most published experts have focused on standard-based reporting, a paucity exists as to how a teacher constructs a grade for the students.

This publication will give teachers a guideline and suggestions for letter grade determination. It clearly defines choices, for teachers, regarding grade construction using standard-based scoring rubrics. In essence, it provides teachers with examples and methods, using scoring rubrics, to properly determine student learning and transfer that learning into a grade.

Note:

Whether it is Common Core standards or Next Generation standards, this book will help with scoring and grade construction.

The standards used in this publication and in the complete Standard-Based Classroom Guide Series has been taken from the Washington State Office of Public Instruction website, www.k12.wa.us.

References:

O'Conner, K. (2009). *How to Grade for Learning K-12* (3rd Ed.), Corwin, Thousand Oaks, CA.

Guskey, Thomas R., and Bailey, Jane M., (2010) *Developing Standard-Based Report Cards*. Thousand Oaks, CA: Corwin.

Stiggins, Richard J. (2006). *Assessment for Learning: A Key to Motivation and Achievement*. Edge.

CHAPTER 1:
WHAT IS STANDARD BASED GRADING?

> **Standard-Based Instruction is teaching, using an organizational system of learning, based on the four.**

Standard-based grading is a system of grading based on a four-point scale where every learning goal or target is taken from state standards. Grades are not averaged; instead medians or modes are the method of calculation. **Standard-based reporting** is the construction of a report card using the standard-based grading system. **Standard-based teaching or instruction** is teaching, using an organizational system of learning, based on the four point scale. Everything from assignments, study guides, journaling and assessments are layered according to the four-point scale. Using this four-point scale, a letter grade is assigned from a grade scale.

> **Everything from assignments, study guides, journaling and assessments are layered according to the four-point scale.**

Standard-based grading has been defined by Tomlinson and McTighe (2006). These six principles are:

1. <u>Grades should be based on clearly specified learning goals and performance standards.</u> Grades are based on academically important goals. Most districts use the state developed targets for these goals.

2. <u>Evidence used for grading should be valid.</u> Grades should be calculated from scores that are derived only from learning the communicated goal or target. As an example, penmanship and other non-target related factors are not used in the grade calculation.

3. <u>Grades should be based on established criteria, not arbitrary norms.</u> Grades are not adjusted to fit a bell curve. Scores are derived solely from assessments measuring content-specific criteria.

4. <u>Not everything should be included in grades.</u> Formative grading is not used in the final grade. Homework, for example, is not summative proof of understanding so should not be put in the grade.

5. <u>Avoid grading based on averages (mean).</u> A score derived from averaging only informs students about how much they did not learn. Score should inform students and teachers alike which concepts have been mastered and which not.

6. <u>Factors such as effort, participation, attendance, homework, etc., should be addressed separately.</u> Factors that are not directly related to the academic target should not be included in a score like participation, attendance, and attitude. While important to the student's education, these factors should be reported separately so that a score clearly shows only a reflection of target mastery.

WHAT IS STANDARD-BASED TEACHING OR INSTRUCTION?

These six principles of Tomlinson and McTighe (2006) are, for the author, the foundation to standard-based grading, reporting and instruction. Using these principles, students and teachers can clearly discuss and evaluate gaps in education and student strengths. **While these principles are foundational, there is virtually nothing to inform a teacher as to how standard-based instruction should advance.**

In **Standard-Based Teaching: A Classroom Guide** (Elder 2012), the following nine elements help teachers to fill in this instructional gap.

> Using these principles, students and teachers can clearly discuss and evaluate gaps in education and student strengths.

THE NINE ELEMENTS OF STANDARD-BASED TEACHING

> The following nine elements help teachers to fill in instructional gaps.

1. **Creating an accurate target for rubric building:**
State standards are often constructed with multiple attributes in a language the student cannot understand. It is imperative that the target be properly constructed for clear communication about learning.

2. **Building a proper rubric:**
Rubrics must be created in levels where logical steps, scaffold learning from foundational learning, bridging knowledge and final target mastery.

3. **Design any unit that supports rubric scaffolding:**
Units need to be designed to teach at each level in the rubric. Using a unit template that is set up for rubric support makes this task far easier for the teacher.

4. **Types of rubric:**
Rubrics can be created for different purposes; the most common type is the single concept rubric. Rubrics can also be designed for processes and procedures.

5. **Organization of a student journal:**
Student journaling is the most effective method of tracking formative assessment of student understanding. Journals are organized in rubric levels and color-coded or numbered accordingly.

6. **Student retrieval of scaffold learning and reflection:**
Study guides must help the student to determine what to review, and how to review it. They should be diagnostic as to whether or not the student has learned targets. Study guide scaffolding also matches all previous scaffolding set up by the rubric.

7. Scaffold assessments:
Like everything taught before it, the learning should be assessed by the levels in the rubric: Foundational (level 1), Bridge to Target (level 2); and Target Proficiency (level 3).

8. Reteach session using a rubric scaffold:
If students are not successful in passing the summative assessment, they are given another chance to master targets, starting with the level the student did not master.

9. Advanced learning:
Some students will need a learning challenge that goes beyond target proficiency. This is advanced learning or level 4. This can be done in a project form, such as an extra advanced assignment per quarter or as regular assessments.

> With the ever changing evaluation systems for teachers, it is important that teachers' learning scores are organized in such a way that they can be used as data for evidence of student learning and teacher evaluation.

These nine elements help teachers to properly chunk learning into understandable and learnable steps. They provide the framework for high-level communication between teacher and student about learning gaps and learning achievements.

These nine elements also provide the organizational framework for data collection. **With the ever changing evaluation systems for teachers, it is important that student assessment scores are organized in such a way that they can be used as evidence of student learning and teacher evaluation.**

All templates for constructing learning using the nine elements above can be found in Standard-Based Teaching: A Classroom Guide (Elder 2012). Some of these templates have also been reproduced in the back of this book.

References:

Elder, Danelle, (2012): *Standard Based Teaching: A Classroom Guide.* http://www.amazon.com/Danelle-Elder-Standard-Based-Teaching/dp/B00N4FR7R2

Tomlinson, C. A., and McTighe, J. (2006). *Integrating Differentiated Instruction and Understanding by Design.* Alexandria, VA: ASCD.

CHAPTER 2:
TARGET AND RUBRIC CONSTRUCTION

Before creating scoring rubrics and grading scales, it is important to construct a proper target.

Targets should be written in student friendly language, with a singular component or attribute (Elder 2012; Guskey and Bailey 2010). Targets should also be written from the perspective of the student, thus empowering the students to learn.

> **Before creating scoring rubrics and grading scales, it is important to construct a proper target.**

Target: Analyze the costs and benefits of decisions which colonists made to meet their needs and wants.

The above standard has multiple components and is not written in student friendly language. It can be made into two different targets.

Target: I can analyze the costs of decisions which colonists made to meet their needs and wants.

Target: I can analyze the benefits of decisions colonists made to meet their needs and wants.

In the above targets, only one component is the focus. Further, it is written in an 'I can' statement. *Costs* and *benefits* of the colonist's address different learning so should be addressed in separate targets.

It is also important to consider the complexity of the desired performance in the target. The target above asks students to *analyze* information about the colonists. When looking at the

Revised Bloom's Taxonomy (Anderson and Krathwohl, 2001), **analysis** is an upper level thinking, performance. See Appendix for the Revised Blooms Taxonomy list.

It is likely because it is upper level thinking, that there was previous learning about colonists that preceded this target. For example, students probably needed to previously study the lifestyles of people at that time. It would have been necessary to successfully analyze the costs and benefits of people in the 1400s to 1700s, resource availability and lifestyle along with other aspects, like health and religious beliefs would be necessary. Simply jumping into an analysis level performance for students would be very confusing without first teaching the background knowledge for this topic.

To understand more about developing appropriate targets see Standard-Based Teaching: A Classroom Guide (Elder 2012).

RUBRIC CONSTRUCTION

> These proficiencies are determined as a dichotomous decision, a pass or fail determination

Creating a scoring rubric is a four step process. Each step or scaffold is a performance that students need to successfully pass, showing mastery at each level. These proficiencies are determined as a **dichotomous decision**, a pass or fail determination (Guskey and Bailey, 2010) of student learning. How these levels are scored is explained later in this publication.

For help constructing a proper scaffold rubric, the teacher can use the revised edition of Bloom's Taxonomy (Anderson 2001) see Appendix. **Each level progresses in learning with level 3 as target proficiency.**

If students pass simpler levels and fail advanced levels then it is clear to both student and teacher where the student needs more practice and assistance.

When teachers plan units, they must first construct a proper target and then a proper rubric. These are some essential questions that may help the teacher construct a scoring rubric:

> When teachers plan units, they must first construct a proper target and then a proper rubric.

- What is the foundational learning for this target?
- What is the progression of learning to reach target mastery?
- What is the proficient level of learning the student must master?
- What advanced learning should be associated with the target mastery?

RUBRIC TYPES

A single concept rubric is the most common rubric used in the classroom. This is where a single target is the focus of learning. A rubric where a student is assessed on a single goal per unit or time period is called a **product** rubric (Guskey and Bailey 2010). This is the rubric type that will be the focus of this publication.

> A properly constructed rubric only has one concept as a target.

A properly constructed target only has one concept as a target. If more than one concept needs to be taught simultaneously, then a **multi-target rubric** must be used.

For more information on multi-target and other rubric types not covered in this publication see Standard-Based Teaching: A Classroom Guide (Elder, 2012).

THE FOUR LEVELS OF A RUBRIC

Before examining some properly constructed scoring rubrics, it can be helpful to consider a non-example of a scoring rubric. Too often teachers construct rubrics that only mirror the traditional mean system of grading. Because there is much pressure to change grading practices with little instruction as to how to do this, it is not surprising that teachers may construct a rubric incorrectly.

They are not the only ones! Many, many curriculums and educational experts have done the same thing, believing they are providing standard-based instruction with built-in scoring rubrics. The example below provides a look at the most common error in rubric construction.

Figure 1

Example of an Improperly Constructed Rubric

Level 1	Level 2	Level 3	Level 4
The students got a few of the punctuations correct	The student got some of the punctuations correct	The student got most of the punctuation correct	The student got all the punctuation correct

Figure 2 also shows a common error in writing a rubric.

Figure 2
Another Non-Example of Rubric Construction

Level 1	Level 2	Level 3	Level 4
The students missed 5-6 of the punctuation corrections	The student missed 3-4 of the punctuation corrections	The student missed 1-2 punctuation corrections	The student got all the punctuations correct

Negatively Constructed Rubric:

They begin with the target at level 3 then reduce student's scores for missing content.

Positively Constructed Rubric:

Each level builds on the other until the target is reached.

In both Figures 1 and 2, the rubric's target is correctly positioned at level 3. However, both of these rubrics are examples of a **Negative Rubric Construction**. These rubrics begin with the target at level 3, then reduce student's scores for missing content. Also, there is no significant difference for the advanced level assessment (level 4) compared to the target (level 3) in this example. Missing a few points on an assessment (level 3) and getting all punctuation correct show the same thing: learning mastery of the target. These differences are insignificant. There is no level change between them.

Looking at both level 1 and 2 where students miss a significant amount of points on an assessment only provides information about one thing…the student did not reach mastery. Levels 1 and 2 relate to the target learning. Neither shows any subordinate understanding of the target and so should not be scored separately.

Figure 3 shows a **Positively Constructed Rubric**. The rubric is built on the content, ending with the target at level 3 and advanced understanding at level 4.

Figure 3

Rubric Levels of Learning

Incomplete Evidence of Learning (I)	Level I: Foundation For Target	Level 2: Progress Toward Target Proficiency	Level 3: Target Proficiency	Level 4: Advanced Application of Target

When the rubric is built properly (Figure 3), it changes from simple foundational understanding (level 1) to advanced understanding of the target learning (level 4). Each level builds on the previous level to create a deeper understanding based on a state standard.

Level 1: The Foundation

According to Ruby Payne (2005), teaching vocabulary creates the most equitable prospect for students' future progress. Vocabulary allows students to master the use of resources online for in texts, confidence applying for jobs and preparing for interviews and many other skills that help create success. By graduation, lower socioeconomic students are often missing thousands of words in their vocabulary, when compared to their middle and upper socioeconomic counterparts. These students are usually not performing well on state assessments.

When trying to learn target knowledge, if students are missing needed vocabulary, they can become hesitant and confused. How is it possible for student to successfully pass an assessment based on a state standard when students can't understand the meaning of that standard due to a lack of vocabulary understanding?

> **Vocabulary is the foundation for many targets or standards.**

Vocabulary becomes the foundation for many targets or standards. It can be woven into the beginning of the unit and taught as words present themselves in the unit. Depending on the teacher's style or students' learning style, teaching vocabulary greatly improves the chances the student will pass the assessment.

Vocabulary can be learned using any number of activities, from games to rote learning. There are a plethora of vocabulary software that are easy to use and create multiple activities for students. Foldables for students to color and diagram is the author's favorite vocabulary building activity.

To learn how students use these activities when journaling see Standard-Based Journaling: A Classroom Guide (2015). Journaling is a power tool the student can use to distinguish and learn each level.

> **Starting units with vocabulary is an easy way for every student to succeed.**

It is important that students be successful when starting a unit. Starting units with vocabulary is an easy way for every student to succeed. Skills needed to learn vocabulary are useful outside the classroom too. These very skills arm students with strategies to learn necessary job-related information. Andrew Cohen (2014) calls this strategy **confidence-based repetition**.

Figure 4

Correct Example of a Rubric

Incomplete Evidence of Learning (I)	Level I: Foundation For Target	Level 2: Progress Toward Target Proficiency	Level 3: Target Proficiency	Level 4: Advanced Application of Target
No evidence of meeting standard	I can define or diagram a: • negative number • positive number • plot • whole numbers • decimals • graph	I can plot both negative and positive numbers	I can accurately graph both negative and positive numbers	I can graph both negative and positive decimal numbers

Six to eight words provides enough content for a unit as well as, creates a learnable list of words that is not daunting to the student. More seems to add anxiety. Beginning a unit where students are anxious can be a death sentence to learning.

Level 2: The Bridge

Level 2 is usually a simpler concept that builds towards the more complicated target. The bridge concept is developed by thinking about the first thing students need to know about the target.

In Figure 4, making sure students understand the concept of negative and positive whole numbers is paramount to graphing them. So it naturally falls between the vocabulary (level 1) which is the foundation for the target and the target proficiency (level 3).

The author prefers level 2 to be assessed using the student's journal. **Checking student journals for understanding at least once a unit helps maintain student accountability.**

Level 3: Target Proficiency

Level 3 is target proficiency. This target should be taken directly from state standards when possible. State standards are written for educator use. Rewording is often required to ensure that students understand target language. As previously stated, the target must be written as a singular component target.

> Rewording is often required to ensure that students understand target language.

Level 4: Advanced Understanding

Level 4 understanding goes beyond the target at level 3. Geiser (2004) states that students should challenge themselves opting for more rigorous coursework. When students regularly strive to learn more than what is required, colleges and universities see these students as highly qualified. They seek to attract these students to attend their institutions. It follows that students should be given higher-level thinking opportunities in k-12 classrooms.

Some students believe they will not continue their education beyond high school. When these students achieve level 4 proficiency, it gives them self-confidence and may motivate them to further their education.

There is much conversation among teachers about this level. Simply going beyond the target does not ensure that advanced learning is occurring. The learning must be tied to the target, as well as adding content to the target that creates more complicated learning.

There are a couple ways this level can be constructed:

1) by moving up in Blooms descriptors
2) by combining the target with a new content area.

As an example, if the target requires a student to create a haiku about spring for an English class, an advanced level might be combining an historical point to the haiku where spring is mentioned. Another example may be asking students to research a specific location in the spring and incorporate that into their haiku. An advanced level then could be asking students to write a haiku about spring in the Rocky Mountains.

> Achieving a 100% score is not advanced learning.

Looking at another content, if the target is a science target then adding a math component creates an advanced learning and so is level 4.

Grading a set of questions about the target on an assessment, then giving advanced credit because the student got a perfect score, is not advanced learning.

If mastery is accomplished at a correct score of 80%, achieving a 100% score is **not** advanced learning. Advanced learning comes only from concepts that advance the target into a more complicated and upper level thinking. There is very little learning difference between getting 4/5 correct or 5/5 correct. The score 5/5 is not advanced learning…it is not more complicated. It is not upper level learning so it should not be placed at level 4 in the rubric.

See Appendix for Rubric Construction Template.

USING THE REVISED BLOOMS TAXONOMY

The Revised Blooms Taxonomy (Anderson, 2001) can be seen in the Figure 5 below.

Figure 5

Revised Blooms Taxonomy by

Anderson and Krathwohl's Taxonomy 2001

Revised Blooms:
1. Remembering
2. Understanding
3. Applying
4. Analyzing
5. Evaluating
6. Creating

1. Remembering: Recognizing or recalling knowledge from memory by using definitions, facts, or lists, or recitation as evidence of learning.

2. Understanding: Demonstrating meaning by preforming interpretation, classification, summarization, inferring, comparing, graphing and explaining as evidence of learning.

3. Applying: Execution of a procedure. Applying knowledge to situations of learned material by using models, reports, sketches, presentations, interviews or diagramming as evidence of learning.

4. Analyzing: Dividing a concept into pieces, determining how these pieces relate to one another through differentiation, organization or comparing by using spreadsheets, surveys, charts, diagrams or graphic representations as evidence of learning.

5. Evaluating: Making judgments based on criteria and standards through checking and critiquing by using recommendations, testing or defending conclusions as evidence of learning.

6. Creating: Designing or putting elements together to form a functional or working whole to create a new pattern or structure through generating, planning or inventing as evidence of learning.

By looking at this revised taxonomy, teachers can scaffold a rubric properly.

By using the Taxonomy Selection Template teachers can craft a well-structured and properly differentiated rubric (Figure 6).

Because there are only four levels in a rubric, only four taxonomy levels can be selected as evidence of learning.

The process for using the Taxonomy Selection Template is:

- A target based on a state standard is selected.
- Then verbs are chosen based on the Revised Blooms Taxonomy for each level of the rubric.
- The level is assigned to each chosen verb or action.
- Finally the description for each rubric level is constructed.

Sometimes state standards are complex and so it can be helpful to use the Taxonomy Selection Template when trying to determine the complexity of the verb or descriptor at each level.

Figure 6

Taxonomy Selection Template

Target: I can explain how each part of the government is connected to the other.

Revised Blooms Taxonomy Level	Verb Associated With Revised Blooms Level	Chosen Rubric Level Associated With Verb	Rubric Level Description
Creating			
Evaluating	Defend or Critique	Level 4	I can defend or critique the system of checks and balances which prevents one branch from gaining too much power.
Analyzing			
Applying	Diagram	Level 3	I can diagram how each part of the government is connected to the other.
Understanding	Explain	Level 2	I can explain how each branch has its own responsibilities and powers.
Remembering	Define vocabulary	Level 1	I can define: • Executive Branch • Judicial Branch • Legislative Branch • Congress • Senate • House of Representatives • Supreme Court • President

This template can be found in the Appendix.

Using the taxonomy selection template, teams and departments can agree on what will be assessed while still giving the teacher freedom to choose activities and assessments.

References:

Anderson, L. W. & Krathwohl, D.R. (Eds.) (2001). Taxonomy for Learning, Teaching, and Assessing: A Revision of Bloom's Taxonomy of Educational Objectives. New York: Addison Wesley Longman.

Cohen, Andrew, Modified on August 12, 2014, https://www.brainscape.com/blog/2011/04/rote-memorization-important/

Elder, Danelle, (2012): *Standard Based Teaching: A Classroom Guide.* http://www.amazon.com/Danelle-Elder-Standard-Based-Teaching/dp/B00N4FR7R2

Geiser, Saul, Santelices, Veronica, (2004), *The Role of Advanced Placement and Honors in Higher Education*. Center for Studies in Higher Education, University of California, Berkeley California

Guskey, Thomas R., Bailey, Jane M. (2010). Developing Standard-based Report Cards. Thousand Oaks, CA: Corwin

Payne, R. K., (2005) A Framework for Understanding Poverty (4th Ed.). Highlands, TX:RFT Publishing

CHAPTER 3:
PROBLEMS WITH THE TRADITIONAL MEAN SYSTEM OF GRADING

THE MEAN SYSTEM OF GRADING ASSESSMENTS

In the traditional mean system of grading, the process for assigning a grade is usually as follows:

1. The teacher arbitrarily chooses a number of problems for the assessment. Each problem's worth an arbitrary point value.

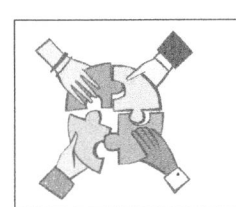

2. Totaling up all the points from each problem, the teacher would change the points into a percentage.

3. Then that percentage would be compared to the percentage cut-off to determine the student's letter grade.

4. Then the student would be assigned a grade.

To examine the validity of the traditional mean system of grading consider the example below:

Generic Example of Assessment Grading:

In the following example there are 6 problems and each problem is worth three points (Figure 7). The total test is worth 18 points. So, 18 point equals 100% of the total test value. The criteria for scoring is 90-100%= A, 80-89%= B, 70-79%=C, 60-69%=D. If a student misses two problems then the score is 12 points or 67%. In this case, **the student actually shows mastery of four out of six problems but receives a D grade.**

Figure 7

Assessment Outcome

1. CORRECT +3
2. CORRECT +3
3. INCORRECT -3
4. CORRECT +3
5. CORRECT +3
6. INCORRECT -3

_____

Total= 12/18

It is important to look at why the student missed two problems when determining mastery understanding. As mentioned earlier, the student shows they understood the content area in four different examples. Those four examples are not the focus of the letter grade. **The focus of the grade are the two problems the student missed.**

Because the traditional mean system is 'top heavy', it is weighted from the 100% down. Everything is subtracted from 100% to determine the grade of the student. The grade then reflects only what is missed and not the actual understanding the student shows in the assessment. Credit should be given when students provide evidence they understand, not by the arbitrary value of 100 % minus the total points for wrong answers.

When the student has completed problems showing mastery of the assessed concept and merely receives a D grade, what does the student perceive about their abilities? What happens to the student's attitude when the student believes he/she has been graded unfairly? The student receives a D even though the student has shown four times they clearly understand content knowledge. Use of the mean grading system is antiquated and communicate nothing about learning.

In the scenario below in Figure 8, the student was asked to show understanding about surface area calculation. Two points were awarded for showing student thinking (showing work) and 1 point for the answer. As in the previous assessments the total points for the test is 18 (Figure 8).

Figure 8

Math Assessment Scoring Example

Number of test problems= 6   **(3 points per problem)**

Total points for test = **18 pts**   **18 points =100%**

Total test score of student =**12/18**   **(student missed six points)**

In this example above, Figure 8, the student again has been given a D when missing 6 points out of 18 total.

Figure 9 is a test the math teacher gave this student. The assessment is not designed to show that the student understands any pre-cursory knowledge regarding surface area calculation, only the target, surface area knowledge.

The teacher's notes at the right side in darker ink.

Figure 9

Surface Area Assessment Using the Mean System

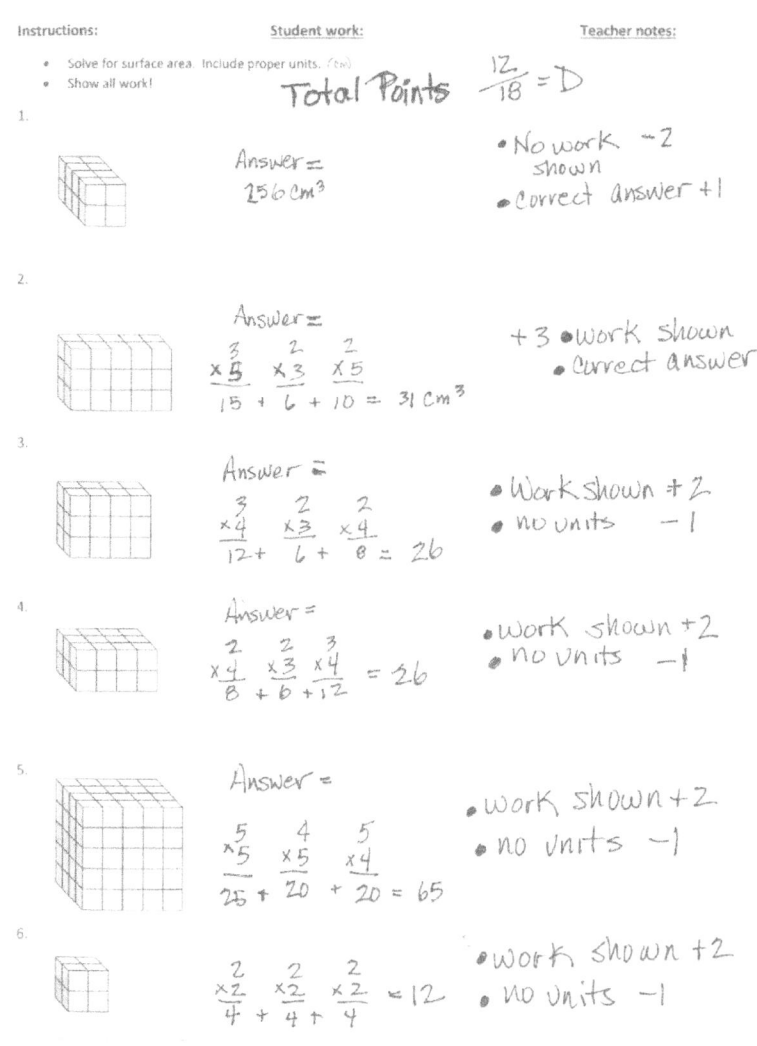

Looking at the actual test scoring, the student knew the process for the calculation of surface area. The student had points deducted on problem 1 for not showing work. In problems 3-6 the student was penalized for not including units in the answer. Therefore the student was given a D.

However, the student correctly shows how to set up surface area calculations. The student correctly calculates the surface area.

Ultimately, the student receives a D. The message this sends to the student is that the student does not understand the concept of calculating surface area, a discouraging message.

This shows perfectly the problem with the traditional mean grading system. It sends the wrong message to the student and teacher both. It feels inherently unfair to the student. It discourages the students, confusing them as to exactly the meaning of success and failure. There is no information as to what knowledge the student has acquired and no information about what they still need to learn.

> Using the traditional mean system combined with a state required target is not standard-based teaching.

The teacher, after looking at the assessment, indicates that the student does not understand how to calculate surface area when in actuality the student does. The teacher may well feel that they are using standard-based teaching method with a state standard to guide their target. Without the proper scaffolding, simply using a state standard as a target does not on its own provide more information for student understanding. Using the traditional mean system combined with a state required target is **not** standard-based teaching.

Using the organizational system presented in **Standard-Based Teaching: A Classroom Guide** (Elder 2012), the student receives a completely different message. Additionally, the teacher has an enlightened understanding of the needs of the student.

Let's look at that same scenario under this system.

First, **a proper target must be established.**

For Washington State, the standard for calculating surface area for middle school students is:

WA.7.3. Core Content: Surface area and volume (Geometry/Measurement) Students extend their understanding of surface area and volume to include finding surface area and volume of cylinders and volume of cones and pyramids. They apply formulas and solve a range of problems involving three-dimensional objects, including problems people encounter in everyday life, in certain types of work, and in other school subjects. With a strong understanding of how to work with both two-dimensional and three-dimensional figures, students build an important foundation for the geometry they will study in high school.

The standard above is far too complicated for teachers to use, will annotate target. The standard covers too much content. Several targets can be constructed from it. One target that can be constructed from the above state standard is:

The student will calculate the surface area of a rectangular prism.

A portion of the standard addresses of volume. It should be taught separately and not included with surface area teaching.

The selected standard has only one concept in it and is simply written. Understanding targets should empower students to learn. Using an 'I can' statement directs students to read the standard and think about it internally and positively.

Converting from the traditional mean grading system to standard-based system is not just a change in the percentages a teacher uses to assess learning. It is also affects the basis for the development of assignments and assessments.

Assuming the teacher has properly constructed a goal or target, the next step is to construct a proper rubric. As previously explained, there are four levels to a proper rubric.

The author uses target supporting vocabulary as the primary choice for Level 1 content (Figure 10).

Figure 10

Surface Area Rubric

Incomplete Evidence of Learning (I)	Level I: Foundation For Target	Level 2: Progress Toward Target Proficiency	Level 3: Target Proficiency	Level 4: Advanced Application of Target
	I can define the following: • cm • cm^3 • length of a rectangular prism • height of a rectangular prism • width of a rectangular prism • faces of a prism	For a rectangular prism, I can calculate: • front of prism • top of prism • side of prism	I can add up all the sides to find the surface area of a rectangular prism	I can draw two rectangular prisms that are congruent with each other

Using the rubric in Figure 10, the assessment is radically different. It is constructed with four different levels. Each level of the assessment linked to each level of the rubric.

Figure 11

Surface Area Assessment Using Standard-Based Teaching Method

Level 1

Define the following: **(each with one point)**

1. cm^3
2. length of a rectangular prism
3. height of a rectangular prism
4. width of a rectangular prism
5. faces of a prism

Level 2

Calculate each side of these prism. Show all work.

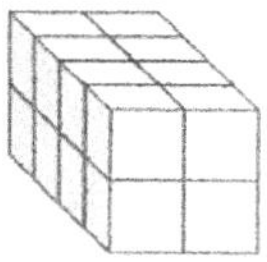

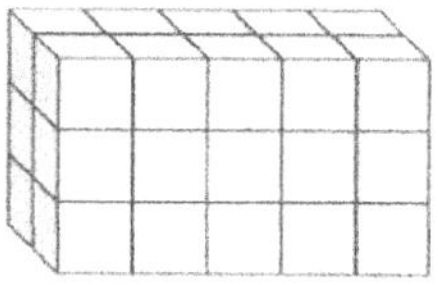

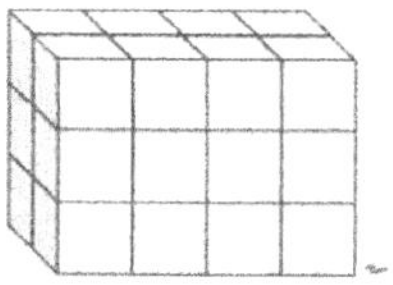

Level 3
Calculate the surface area of the rectangular prisms above. Show all work.
1.

2.

3.

Level 4
Draw two rectangular prisms that are congruent with each other.

In the assessment, Figure 11, each level of the scoring rubric has a corresponding level assessment as a level of the assessment. Level 1 of the rubric has a matching content level 1 assessment. Level 2 of the rubric has a matching content level 2 assessment, etc.

> The scoring rubric and the assessment match identically.

There is no deviation in the assessment from the scoring rubric. The scoring rubric and the assessment match identically. It is important to note that all activities, study guides and assignments are also matched to the scoring rubric. **Furthermore, nothing is taught or assessed that is not supported first by the standard target and then by the scoring rubric.**

In this way there is never a question about what will be assessed. The student knows exactly the progression of the assessment. Also, and most importantly, **both the student and teacher know what concepts have been mastered and what have not.** It is this exact communication that allows the student and teacher to talk in a meaningful way about learning.

Now when the student misses an assessment question, the teacher and the student know exactly where the problem areas lie. At this point, the teacher can assign more work, discuss the problems and help the students to figure out what the next step is to learning.

For the author, a student must show they completed the necessary studying before a reassessment is given for any level. Because level 4 is advanced learning, the student must complete this level correctly the first time it is assessed.

Using this method to organize teaching, the author's state assessment scores among her students have dramatically risen. Further, this method is supported in the Marzano (2012) assessment framework and others.

Looking at a different content, let's consider and language arts assessment. The teacher always needs to start with a proper target and then build the scoring rubric.

Target: **I can write sentences using proper punctuation.**

Looking at Figure 12, there are 6 vocabulary words in level 1 that are critical for understanding the target (level 3):

I can write sentences using proper punctuation.

The proper use of capital letters (Level 2) is a lesser concept than the target. It should be easier and a sub-concept of level 3. Level 4 is advanced, where a student must write a paragraph rather than a statement using proper punctuation.

Figure 12

Example Language Arts Rubric

Incomplete Evidence of Learning (I)	Level I: Foundation For Target	Level 2: Progress Toward Target Proficiency	Level 3: Target Proficiency	Level 4: Advanced Application of Target
	I can give an example of each: • Comma • Exclamation Point • Question Mark • Period • Capital Letter • Lower Case Letter	I can write sentences with the proper use of capital letters	I can write sentences using proper punctuation	I can write a complete paragraph using proper punctuation and capitalization

Looking at the associated assessment (Figure 13), there is a perfect match with the rubric content (Figure 12).

In Figure 13, it is easy to see that the rubric provided to the student at the beginning of a unit correlates directly with the assessment given to a student at the end of a unit. Every assignment, every quiz, every lab or study guide in between follows the same organization. The student is taught and can identify each levels of discrete knowledge. To know more about this unit alignment, see **Standard-Based Teaching: A Classroom Guide (Elder, 2012).**

Figure 13

Punctuation Assessment Using Standard Based Method

Level 1: *Give an example of each:* 1. Comma: 2. Explanation Point: 3. Question Mark: 4. Capital Letter: 5. Lower Case Letter: 6. Punctuation:
Level 2: *Properly capitalize each sentence.* 1. my mother likes flowers. 2. do you know where the school is? 3. she took the bus home.
Level 3: *Add the proper punctuation and capitalization for each sentence.* 1. how many kittens are in the picture 2. my sister is very tall 3. ouch that hurt
Level 4: *Write a three sentence paragraph using the proper punctuation and capitalization.*

Music and the arts are no exception when it comes to standard-based teaching.

Example Music Assessment

The target is:

The student will play the first three phrases of the music 'Take a Moment' fluidly.

Figure 14

Music Performance Rubric

Incomplete Evidence of Learning (I)	Level I: Foundation For Target	Level 2: Progress Toward Target Proficiency	Level 3: Target Proficiency	Level 4: Advanced Application of Target
	I can identify all the notes in the first three phrases of the music	I can tap out the timing of the first three phrases of the music	I can play the first three phrases of the music fluidly	I can play the first three phrases of the music with feeling (using the music notation)

Since this is a performance assessment, the teacher will need to set up criteria about how many attempts the student will be allowed and how many mistakes will be accepted for each level. This is an example of level 1 that is not vocabulary based.

The target is playing the first three phrases of the music fluidly. To support that goal, level 1 states the student will be able to identify all the notes in the first three lines that be able to tap out the timing of these measures (level 2). In the end, the student is individually assessed on four separate chucks of knowledge regarding the selected music.

These examples show an organizational system that is extremely different than the system use in the traditional mean system of grading. First, the rubric is given ahead of the unit so the student knows exactly what will be taught and assessed. Second, the teacher does not deviate from the rubric. The teacher doesn't necessarily need to teach the unit in the order of the rubric but must cull any content that is not part of the rubric learning.

Now, referring to the Standard-Based Teaching method, when a student doesn't successfully pass a level of understanding, two things occur that is perceived as inherently fair to the student. First, the student knows immediately what content the student did not master. Secondly, the student gets credit for the content the student did master.

Reference:

Elder, Danelle, (2012): *Standard Based Teaching: A Classroom Guide.* http://www.amazon.com/Danelle-Elder-Standard-Based-Teaching/dp/B00N4FR7R2

Marzano, R. J., and others (2012). *Becoming a Reflective Teacher.* Bloomington, IN: Marzano Research Laboratory.

Washington State K–12 Learning Standards (2015): State of Washington, Office of Public Instruction, https://www.k12.wa.us/curriculuminstruct/

CHAPTER 4:
STANDARD BASED SCORING

> **Scoring rubric** determines the level of understanding in a unit.
>
> **Grading scale** determines the procedure were settled scores are evaluated and a grade is assigned.

For clarity purposes, instead of using the term grading rubric, a *grading scale* will be used whenever an actual grade is assigned. It's important to clearly understand that a **scoring rubric** is used to determine the level of understanding in a unit. A **grading scale** is a grade determining procedure where several scores are evaluated and based on this scale, and grade is assigned.

When formulating a scoring rubric, as an individual teacher, team, school, or district, decisions must be made first about the level of academic rigor that grades will reflect. Decisions must be made as to what each grade will communicates to the students, parents and educators.

For example, one of the first decisions may be:

- how many levels should the scoring rubric have
- what value should be assigned per level
- where the target learning should be placed inside the rubric.

There are many websites that are available for teachers to construct rubrics.

Guskey and Bailey (2010), *Developing Grading Reporting Systems for Student,* set the target at a performance level 3 out of 4 performance levels. This is the author's preference as well.

Also, O'Conner (2009), 'How to Grade for Learning K-12' gives example after example of various school district data where the standard is set at the third level in a scoring rubric.

Scoring student papers with a scoring rubric is simpler than scoring papers using the traditional mean system of grading. It is reported as an up or down finding. In other words, it's a

dichotomous decision (Guskey, 2010). For each learning level, the assessments are scored as pass/fail.

Let's look at an example.

Figure 15

Surface Area Rubric

Incomplete Evidence of Learning (I)	Level I: Foundation For Target	Level 2: Progress Toward Target Proficiency	Level 3: Target Proficiency	Level 4: Advanced Application of Target
	I can define the following: • cm • cm^2 • length of a rectangular prism • height of a rectangular prism • width of a rectangular prism • faces of a prism	I can calculate: • front of prism • top of prism • side of prism	I can add up all the sides to find the surface area of a rectangular prism	I can draw two rectangular prisms that are congruent with each other

In Figure 15, Surface Area Rubric, the target or level 3 understanding is calculating the total surface area. The student starts with learning the vocabulary (level 1) for this unit. Next, the student needs to learn to add up all the sides of the rectangle (level 2) as the next step before tackling the target (level 3).

In Figure 16, the student has taken the surface area assessment. In level 1 of the assessment, the student did not answer one of the definitions. The student, in this case, has shown understanding in four other. At this level, 4 out of 5 correct answers shows mastery of the vocabulary definitions for this unit. So the student passes level 1.

Figure 16

Student Example of Surface Area Assessment

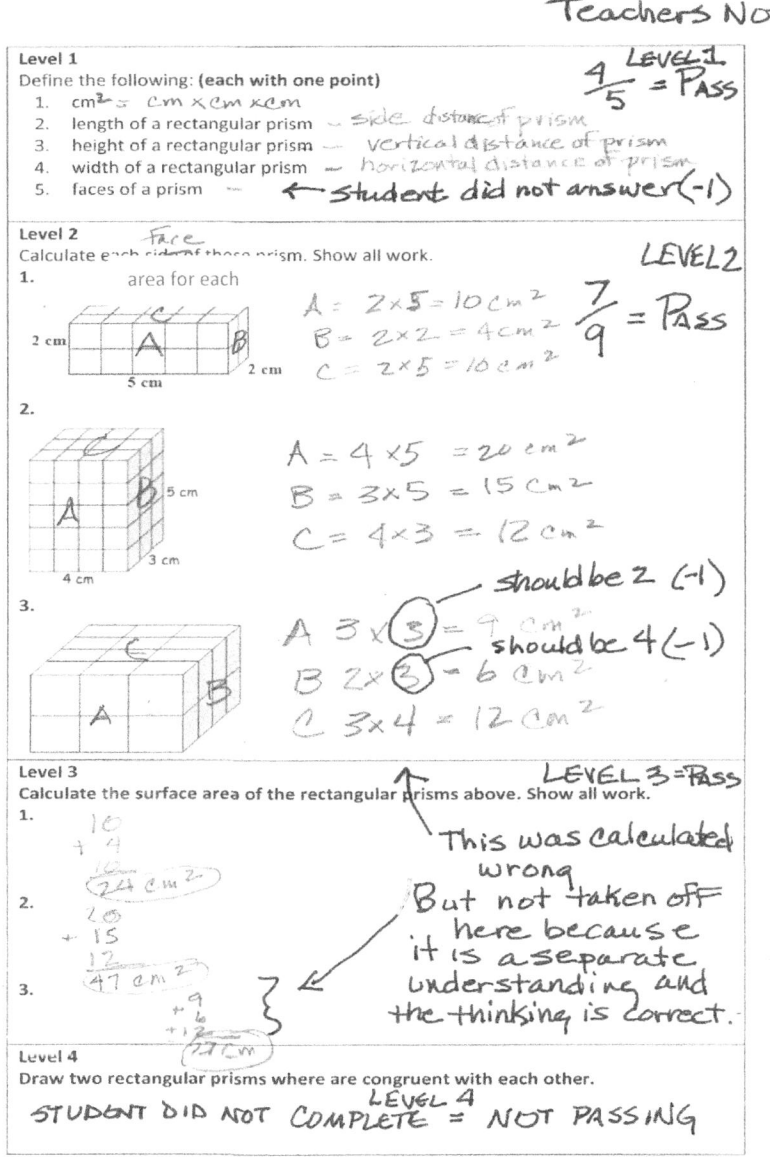

In this assessment, the teacher's notes are in darker handwriting on the right. The student has incorrectly counted squares in the third problem of level 2, but still shows mastery of the content. The student passes level 2.

In level 3, the student takes the erroneous calculations from level 2, and uses them to calculate total surface area. Because it is a separate understanding, it is graded separately. No points are taken away for these mistakes from the previous level. Therefore, the student passes level 3.

Student did not complete the level 4 portion of the assessment. Therefore the student does not pass this level.

> **Using a rubric to set up an assessment allows the student to receive the most information about mastery.**

Using a rubric to set up an assessment allows the student to receive the most information about mastery learning. From the above assessment, both the student and teacher now know that the target learning (level 3) has been achieved as well as levels 1-2. Regardless of content, organizing assessments by this system scaffolding content allows students and teachers the ability to monitor content mastery.

In another example, Figure 17, the Language Arts assessment is organized exactly like the rubric.

Figure 17

Punctuation Rubric

Incomplete Evidence of Learning (I)	Level I: Foundation For Target	Level 2: Progress Toward Target Proficiency	Level 3: Target Proficiency	Level 4: Advanced Application of Target
	I can give an example of each: • Comma • Exclamation Point • Question Mark • Period • Capital Letter • Lower Case Letter	I can write sentences with the correct use of capital letters	I can write sentences using proper punctuation	I can write a complete paragraph using proper punctuation and capitalization

D. Elder ☒ 2015

In Figure 18, the teacher's notes are in darker ink.

Figure 18

Student Example of Punctuation Assessment

Level 1: Give an example of each:	Teacher Notes:
1. Comma: , 2. Explanation Point: ! 3. Question Mark: ? 4. Capital Letter: (Capital L circled) 5. Lower Case Letter: e 6. Punctuation: . ! ?	ALL CORRECT! PASS LEVEL 1

Level 2: Properly use of capital letters in each sentence.	
1. my mother likes flowers. My mother likes flowers.	ALL CORRECT! PASS LEVEL 2
2. do you know where the school is? Do you know where the school is?	
3. she took the bus home. She took the bus home.	

Level 3: Add the proper punctuation and capital letters for each sentence. 4/4 = NOT PASSING
1. How many kittens are in the picture ? ← I corrected each
2. My sister is very tall . ← sentence so you
3. Ouch that, hurt ! ← could see what you missed

Level 4: write a three sentence paragraph using the proper punctuation.

I like green beans. I like to put cheese on them!

(2/3 - You needed 3 sentences. LEVEL 4 NOT PASSING)

In this assessment, the student passes levels 1 and 2. It is clear from the mistakes student makes in level 3 that the student mastery has not been achieved when asked to the use of all punctuations required. The student passes levels 1 and 2, identify punctuation marks and capitalizing sentences but has not learned the rest of the punctuation usage.

In level 4, the student only provides two out of three sentences to show mastery of writing a paragraph with correct punctuation. The two sentences the student provides are correct. It is up to

> The information gained when using this organizational system is in stark contrast to the information provided from a traditional mean system of grading.

the teacher's discretion to judge whether this is enough evidence to show mastery of this level.

The information gained when using this organizational system, is in stark contrast to the information provided from a traditional mean system of grading. Here the rubric is the heart of all activities and assessments. In this system, the student knows what content needs more attention and what has been learned. The teacher is able to give credit to the student for content where evidence shows mastery.

Once again looking at the previous performance rubric (Figure 19), one can now that with the matching assessment (Figure 20).

Figure 19

Music Performance Rubric

Incomplete Evidence of Learning (I)	Level I: Foundation For Target	Level 2: Progress Toward Target Proficiency	Level 3: Target Proficiency	Level 4: Advanced Application of Target
	I can identify all the notes in the first three phrases of the music	I can tap out the timing of the first three phrases of the music	I can play the first three phrases of the music fluidly	I can play the first three phrases of the music with feeling (using the music direction)

In this assessment (Figure 20), the music teacher has listened to the student play from the required musical score. The teacher has used the music performance rubric to guide their scoring of students learning. Below are the marks and scores the teacher gave the student.

Figure 20

Student Example Assessment For Music Performance Assessment

Music Performance Assessment
Level 1: The student identified all the notes in the three phrases correctly.   Level 1: Pass
Level 2: The student tapped out the timing of the three phrases with minor errors.   Level 2: Pass
Level 3: The student played the three phrases fluidly (without breaks).   Level 3: Pass
Level 4: The student played three phrases using all the music direction.   Level 4: Pass

In the above assessment, scoring, the student correctly shows evidence of learning for each of the four levels.

A simple template is provided in the appendix for test construction.

UNIT ALIGNMENT

A template is provided in the Appendix for teachers to align all parts of a unit. This template is helpful when first developing a standard-based instruction background (Figure 21). It is a good check even for experienced teachers using standard-based instruction.

Figure 21`

Unit Alignment Guide

◊ Students have a Table of Contents which has a column to mark levels.

◊ At the very beginning of a unit, students are given a scoring rubric with each level description.

◊ Students set goals for mastering each level.

◊ Students are given time to use appropriate strategies to study each level.

◊ Students are given simple exit tasks where they evaluate their understanding of a particular level.

◊ Students are given a study guide that has a sample problem for each level.

◊ Students are given an assessment where each level is separate and scored separately.

◊ Students evaluate their success at learning each level.

◊ The teacher enters a **differentiated score** for each level (a separate score which can later be summarized).

◊ The teacher provides a relearning and retesting experience for students on assessment levels that where not mastered when evidence of studying has been presented to the teacher.

Unit alignment guide can help teachers think about unit timing. It is only meant to be used as a reminder teachers about the many opportunities in the classroom to emphasize level learning.

References:

Guskey and Bailey (2010), *Developing Grading Reporting Systems for Student,* Thousand Oaks, CA: Corwin

O'Conner in *How to Grade for Learning K-12* (3rd Ed.), Corwin, Thousand Oaks, CA

CHAPTER 5:

THE CLEAR PROBLEM WITH THE TRADITIONAL MEAN SYSTEM OF GRADING

Asking a teacher to change their grading practice often feels like a very request. It cannot be overstated that replacing a grading system (one that has been used for over a century) is a slow process. The teacher needs opportunity over time for input into this process. The process also needs substantial communication back and forth to all parties involved but particularly from the teacher.

To create change by simply exerting pressure on the teacher will merely create angst and resentment. It might not create the deep and meaningful understanding that a foundational shift of this nature requires. Foundational preparation should be emphasized when planning this type of foundational change. Teachers are encouraged to share this philosophy with their superiors.

> To create change by simply exerting pressure on the teacher will merely create angst and resentment.

To facilitate a change in a teacher's philosophy as deeply rooted as grading, it is necessary to consider what grades have meant to teachers, students and parents for a century.

The word 'average' mathematically means that grades are compared and students in the middle are considered 'average'. Average refers to grading based on a bell shaped curve, where a large number of C's are issued. In the classroom, various grading situations make this statistically not true. Grading patterns do not follow a bell shaped curve would support (Ghezzi, 2014).

When considering the word 'average ', one professor, Stanlick, (2015) from the University of Central Florida interprets a C this way:

C= average, meets minimum expectations and satisfies course requirements.

Looking at other sources, the United States Department of Education (2008) clearly outlines the traditional mean system of grading in Figure 22.

Figure 22

United States Department of Education System of Grading

Norm-Reference Grading System

A (Excellent)	= Top 10 % of Class
B (Good)	= Next 20 % of Class
C (Average, Fair)	= Next 30 % of Class
D (Poor, Pass)	= Next 20 % of Class
F (Failure)	= Bottom 20 % of Class

Criterion-Based Grading system

A (Excellent)	= 95-100	or	90-100
B (Good)	= 85-95	or	80- 90
C (Fair)	= 75-85	or	70- 80
D (Poor)	= 65-75	or	60-70
F (Failure)	= -65	or	-60

Clearly, meeting the minimum requirement is not where we want the majority of America's students to be, whether it is in a K-12 public, private school or university.

The traditional mean system of grading, A through F, was believed to be conceived at Mount Holyoke College in Massachusetts in 1897 (Palmer, 2010). At that time, there was no F but "the dreaded E".

> According to Bailey (1998), the traditional mean system of grading promotes assessments that are indirect and inauthentic.

By some accounts, the traditional mean system grading system was based off the grading system for how the quality of beef was rated.

Regardless whether there is an E or F to mean failure, it is clear American schools are well overdue for a more meaningful grading system.

As educators, we should not be talking about a standard deviation measurement with terminology like 'about average, average or below average'. We need to move away from the communicating that a C grade is considered the 'average'. **Instead, we should be communicating purposeful, clear language about grades that pertain to learning.**

We should be discussing with students, parents and community whether the student has acquired target knowledge proficiency or has not.

According to Bailey (1998), the traditional mean system of grading promotes assessments that are indirect and inauthentic. Law and Eckes (1995) say that this type of grading cannot promote deep understanding but are a 'one-shot, speed-based, and norm-referenced' evaluation of student learning.

This system of grading is not found outside the school setting. Adults are not evaluated this way while on-the-job. When learning new information, adults do not receive an F for only learning the first 59% of job knowledge.

It is time to exchange this negative report system of grading to a system that reports mastery.

O'Connor (2002) lists the difference between a traditional grading system and the standard-based grading system in Figure 23.

Figure 23

Traditional Grading System vs Standard-Based Grading System

Traditional Grading System	Standards-Based Grading System
1. Based on assessment methods (quizzes, tests, homework, projects, etc.). One grade/entry is given per assessment.	1. Based on learning goals and performance standards. One grade/entry is given per learning goal.
2. Assessments are based on a percentage system. Criteria for success may be unclear.	2. Standards are criterion or proficiency-based. Criteria and targets are made available to students ahead of time.
3. Use an uncertain mix of assessment, achievement, effort and behavior to determine the final grade. May use late penalties and extra credit.	3. Measures achievement only OR separates achievement from effort/behavior. No penalties or extra credit given.
4. Everything goes in the grade book - regardless of purpose.	4. Selected assessments (tests, quizzes, projects, etc.) are used for grading purposes.
5. Include every score, regardless of when it was collected. Assessments record the average - not the best - work.	5. Emphasize the most recent evidence of learning when grading.

In the end, the standard-based grading system that forms the basis for the **Standard-Based Classroom Guide Series** is based on **competency-based learning**. In other words, students must master content before moving on to the next concept. It is also **criterion-based learning** where students are assessed on their sin learning progress towards a particular standard. In addition, this, this method of **scaffolding efficiently communicates** to students their current level learning so **rapid targeting of unlearned content** can occur.

Reference:

Bailey, K. M. (1998). *Learning about language assessment: dilemmas, decisions, and directions.* Heinle& Heinle: US.

Ghezzi, Patti, (2015): *How to Interpret Report Cards,* www.schoolfamily.com/school-family-articles/article/10690-how-to-interpret-report-cards

Law, B. & Eckes, M. (1995). *Assessment and ESL.* Peguis publishers: Manitoba, Canada.

O'Connor K (2002). *How to Grade for Learning: Linking grades to standards (2nd ed.). Thousand Oaks, CA: Corwin Press*

Palmer, Brian. *E is for Fail, Aug. 9 2010,*

http://www.slate.com/articles/news_and_politics/explainer/2010/08/e_is_for_fail.html

Stanlick, Nancy, (2015): University of Central Florida https://pegasus.cc.ucf.edu/

United States Department of Education, (2008): *Structure of the U.S. Education System:* **U.S.** *Grading Systems,* http://findit.ed.gov/search?utf8=%E2%9C%93&affiliate=ed.gov&query=grading+scale

CHAPTER 6:
THE SIGNIFICANCE OF 1% OF LEARNING

To further highlight the need for change from this century-old system of grading to a standard-based system, it may help to look at this antiquated system of grading using a pie chart as a spacial representation. Looking at the division of knowledge in this way can help one see how the system and grade is weighted to 'punish' the student for unlearned content rather than informing the learner of what has been learned.

> **The traditional mean system of grading is way to 'punish' the student for unlearned content rather than informing the learner of what has been learned.**

In Figure 24 pie chart shows for the traditional mean system of grading. An A is earned by receiving an average of 100- 90% scores for assessments and other score. No advanced learning is required. A B is received by earning an average of 89-80%, on assessments and other score work. A C is earned by receiving an average of 79-70 on assessments and other score. This breakdown for the traditional mean system of grading depicts well the disproportionate amount of knowledge (59%) that students must acquire before even entering a passing grade of a D. No credit is given for 59% of learning.

Using this system, the student receives a general score whereby the student has no idea what areas of need improvement.

Figure 24

Pie chart of the Traditional Grade System Distribution

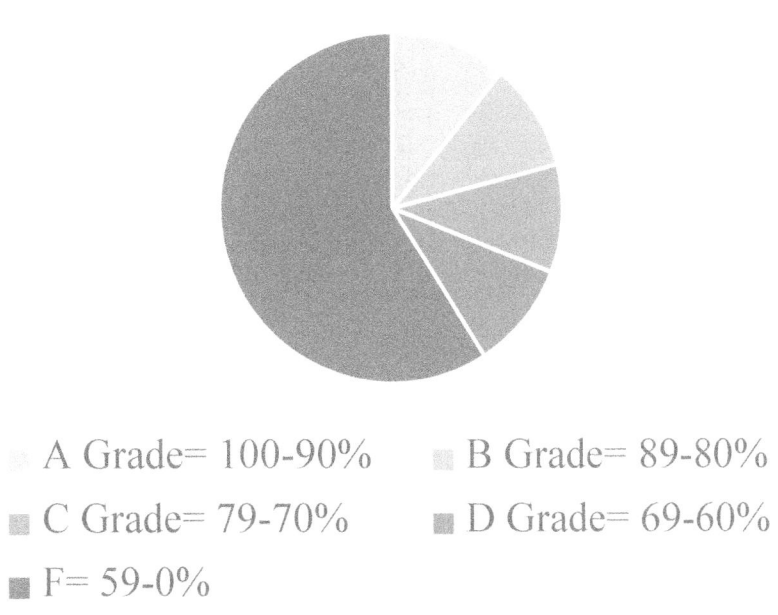

A Grade= 100-90%   B Grade= 89-80%
C Grade= 79-70%   D Grade= 69-60%
F= 59-0%

If we evaluated any other life experience with this system, the inadequacies are more obvious.

In the pie chart, Figure 25, a pre-toddler's walking experience is evaluated using the traditional mean system. Of course, it would be ridiculous to evaluate a child's first walking experience with this method but it begs the question, 'When did we change how we taught children?'

We changed rewarding and encouraging children's learning to judging children with words like 'failure' and 'average'.

Figure 25

Pie Chart of a Child's First Walking Experience

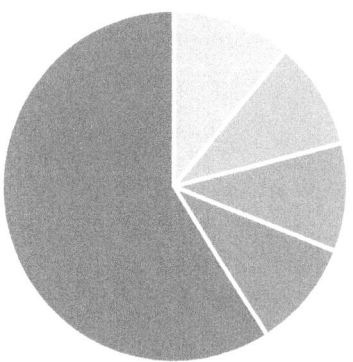

- A= Child walks without falling
- B= Child takes multiple steps
- C= Child takes two steps
- D= Child takes one step
- F= Child can only stand

When looking at percentage distribution for grade construction, the actual grade determination is based on a mere 1% of the total score. When a grade is based on the traditional mean system, the grade is determined not by what one knows but by how much is missed out of 100% to the nearest 1%.

Figure 26

Pie Chart Showing 1% Determination of a Grade

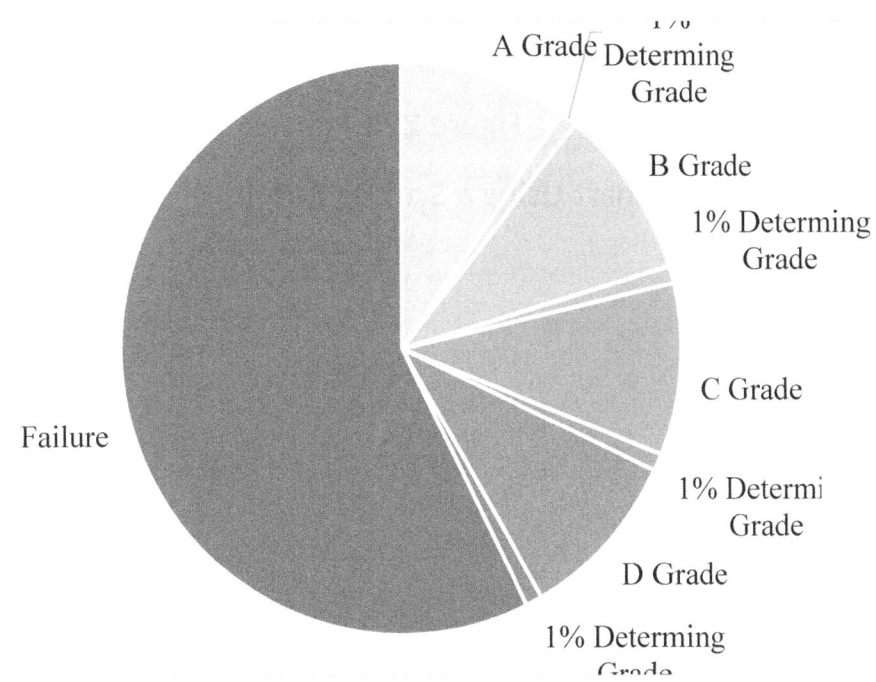

In Figure 26, the mean system is broken down so the grading distribution is visible. In the final analysis, a grade boils down to 1% of learning. One point cannot be truly grasped teacher and students alike. We should be able to explain to students what 1% of learning is since the entire grade depends on it.

The difference between 60% and one less percentage point, 59%, is failure. Educators must be explained this very significant 1%. Students who fail take the entire test again. One percent of learning is not significant when it is the difference between 60% and 61%. That is the same 'leap' as 59% and 60%. Yet for the latter it means failure.

A properly constructed rubric divides the learning into four separate content areas. When a student fails one level, the student gets credit for the levels that were passed, he/she knows exactly what content to study for shown by the levels not passed.

In Figure 27, a pie chart shows the distribution of a scoring rubric.

Figure 27

Pie Chart Using a Scoring Rubric

- Level 1 Content Assessment
- Level 2 Content Assessment
- Level 3 Content Assessment
- Level 4 Content Assessment

In Figure 27, the pie chart shows each section of the scoring rubric is 25% of the score. Also, each level is assessed separately so the teacher and student are aware of the knowledge the student has learned. Because separate credit is given for each level the student is not penalized as in the traditional mean system of grading.

Figure 28

People's Republic of China Map Assessment

1. What is the capital of China?
   a. Beijing
   b. Guangzhou
   c. Harbin
   d. Shanghai
2. Which of the following countries does not border China?
   a. Myanmar
   b. Vietnam
   c. Thailand
   d. India
3. India is north of China.
   a. True
   b. False
4. China is east of Vietnam.
   a. True
   b. False
5. Draw and label in the location of Beijing.
6. China is located in _____.
   a. Africa
   b. Asia
   c. Australia
   d. Europe
7. Approximately how many miles is China at its widest p

D. Elder ☒ 2015

In Figure 28, the student is assessed on the People's Republic of China. The student is evaluated on factual knowledge about China, as well as compass direction questions and a math computational question. These are three separate learning targets and should be separated into different assessments. If a student fails a math computational question and a compass direction questions, it may be true that the student understands perfectly well the facts about China.

Three of the eight question are not relative to the People's Republic of China (questions 2, 3 and 8). Question 2 is a regional question. Learning the names of the countries around China is not **directly** related to a standard that requires a student to learn about China itself. While the point may seem a little gray, it is important to make clear the boundaries of assessment knowledge so that precious classroom time is properly honed in on essential learning.

Question 3 is a directional question and requires students to know the compass directions only. Nothing about China is needed to answer this question.

Question 8 is a distance measurement question. While this is a great skill to learn, if the standard being taught is about China itself, then this question does not fit. Further, asking a single question about direction or distance calculation is not a large enough test sample of understanding to be meaningful. There should be several directional or distance calculation questions to ensure reliability.

If the student missed all three questions that are not about China the student would receive a 62% score…a D.

In other words, the student is penalized for information not related to China…38% of the student's score.

Figure 29

Incorrect Construction of Math Assessment

A. Write as a fraction.
   1. 10^{-3}
   2. 2^{-2}

B. Simplify:
   1. $(2^5 \times 2^3)\, 2^{-2}$
   2. $\dfrac{4^3 \times 4^3}{4^{20}}$

C. Write in exponential form.
   1. $\dfrac{1}{4 \times 4 \times 4}$

   2. $\dfrac{3}{10 \times 10 \times 10 \times 10 \times 10}$

Another example of how traditional mean system of grading penalizes students can be seen in Figure 29. In this assessment, the learning target is vague. The student is evaluated on their understanding of:

- fractions -two questions
- math simplification process- three questions
- writing in the exponential form- two questions

The score is combined into one grade. If the student was successful answering the fraction and simplification questions, but could not correctly answer writing in an exponential form, the student would not be given credit where the student showed understanding for fractions and simplification questions. The student would receive 71%... a C would have failed writing in an exponential while showing mastery fractions and simplification questions.

Grading assessments to each level of learning separately solves the problem of giving a general score for multiple targets.

Looking at a pie chart, Figure 30, students are being assessed on plant growth. The pie chart shows the equal division of scoring for each level of the assessment.

Figure 30

Pie Chart for Example Science Assessment

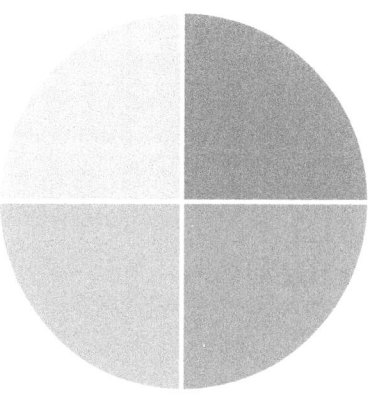

- Level 1: Plant Anatomy Journal Assessment
- Level 2: Plant Anatomy Journal Assessment
- Level 3: Plant Anatomy Journal Assessment
- Level 4: Plant Anatomy Journal Assessment

First, students learn a list of vocabulary words that are associated with the target at level 3, the stages of plant growth.

Looking at Figure 30, the level 3 assessment (target learning), one can see a student could not be successful at describing the succession of a plant from a seed without learning the vocabulary to support that description.

Figure 31

Example of Level 3 Assessment for Plant Growth

Instructions:

Identify the proper stage from 1- 4. Then label the parts for each of the stages.

Stage__ Stage__ Stage__ Stage__

The vocabulary that students need to understand, and use to properly identify the parts of the stages above, are dependent on the grade level of the student.

An example of level one vocabulary for 3rd or 4th grade might be:

- leaf
- root
- seed
- shoot
- stalk

For high school, the supporting vocabulary might be:

- Radicle
- Cotyledon
- Epicotyl
- Plumule
- Stalk
- Testa
- Elongation

This assessment may seem like a level I assessment. However, students are not asked to define or diagram the vocabulary words. Rather, they are asked to use them to determine the stage of each diagram. Both the level 3 concept of plant growth, and the level 1 vocabulary that supports the target of level 3, should be tested and graded separately. Mixing the vocabulary into one score with the target and other levels only confuses what knowledge the student actually should be given credit for and what the student has not successfully mastered.

Any content can be manipulated and leveled to produce discrete, chunked learning in order to develop a proper rubric and assessment.

References:

People's Republic of China Map: Free Printables for K-12 Education, www.studenthandouts.com

Math assessment: imgarcade.com-online image arcade

http://imgarcade.com/1/math-expressions-7th-grade/

CHAPTER 7:
STANDARD-BASED GRADEBOOK ORGANIZATION

When searching for scoring examples on the web, a plethora of sites are available about grade card construction and their meaning. But what about examples and discussions about real gradebook documentation?

Gradebook organization should be set up to reflect the rubric scaffolding. Each level assessed is a dichotomous decision, the student either passes the level or does not. The score entered must reflect this up or down decision simply, a pass or fail.

In the scoring with the standard-based teaching method (Elder, 2012), a single point is awarded when the student passes an assessment level. The point value then for each level is simply 1 or 0. Each level then is worth the same amount of points (one) because each level is a separate learning accomplishment with an up or down determination of success.

> Each level assed is a dichotomous decision, the student either passes the level

This is probably the most difficult shift for teachers. Letting go of all the points and weighted values and substituting instead a simple four point system, can be very difficult culture shift. It is a philosophical change as well as practical move. There is no weighting of grades or complicated formulas. **Only a primary question exists...does the student understand the concept of each level of the rubric?**

It may be best to consider this kind of learning in other life experiences to best understand how a pass or fail system of scoring works.

> Only a primary question exists... Does the student understand the concept of each level of the rubric?

When children are taught to write the alphabet or numbers, the evaluation of whether or not they have learned a letter or number is to have them write it correctly. It is a simple performance assessment. At that point the teacher must decide if the student is successful. The student can either write it properly or they cannot. There is no in between. The teacher cannot say that a student wrote the letter 'A' fifty percent correct.

For a more complicated example, think about taking a driver's test. The test is scored and the person taking the test either passes or fails.

It simplifies learning for the student and scoring for the teacher when grades are assigned this way. There is no way for the student to 'scoot by' and no way for a teacher's subjectivity to get involved.

With this system of scoring, discussions with students become very transparent and meaningful. Students talk about learning to teachers...NOT grade values. This is a huge shift away from counting points and toward a learning target the student and teacher.

Consider an example gradebook full of assessments that were constructed based on well-written targets and rubrics. In this case, the teacher matched the assignments, study guides and assessments to each level of the rubric Figure 32.

Figure 32

Organization of Gradebook by Rubric Levels

Level 1: Civil War Vocabulary Assessment	Level 2: Civil War Journal Assessment	Level 3: Civil War Target Assessment	Level 4: Civil War Advanced Assessment	Level 1: World War 1 Vocabulary Assessment	Level 2: World War 1 Journal Assessment	Level 3: World War 1 Target Assessment	Level 4: World War 1 Advanced Assessment
1	1	1	0	1	1	0	0

Level 1: World War 2 Vocabulary Assessment	Level 2: World War 2 Journal Assessment	Level 3: World War 2 Target Assessment	Level 4: World War 2 Advanced Assessment
1	1	1	0

Looking at the gradebook above, Figure 32, one can see that all three level 1 assessments are vocabulary-based. Level 2 assessments are journal based; Level 3 target; level 4 advanced learning.

This format is the one the author prefers to use in the classroom if the unit being learned has other foundation requirements.

In the gradebook example above, the scores reflect the knowledge stated in the rubric. The student passes the Civil War assessments, levels 1-3, but fails the advanced level 4. For the World War 1 assessments, the student passes levels 1 and 2 but fails 3 and 4.

This method of organizing scores clearly shows to both student and teacher, what standards has been mastered and what has not. Compare the information the teacher and the student receive about learning when looking at the traditional gradebook organization below. Very little can be learned from the score of the traditional mean system other than a very broad confirmation of a general understanding of the assessed content.

Figure 33

Traditional System of Organizing Gradebook

Civil War Assessment	World War 1 Assessment	World War 2 Assessment
81%	74%	82%

> Traditional grading system: In this grading system, the knowledge that has not been learned is valued more than the knowledge of what has been.

In Figure 32, a traditional gradebook, the student gets one score for an entire unit assessment. The student gets no information on what content they successfully learned and what content needs more study. In this system of grading, the knowledge that has **not** been learned is valued more (mathematically) than the **knowledge of what has been learned. The score that is supposed to reflect learning (the evidence of learning), is reduced because** of missed problems. The learner's grade is determined by starting with 100% and subtracting missed points.

Examining the Standard-Based Grading system presented in this book, it is easy for a teacher to explain to a parent or a student the significance of a single point. It means either the student understood the content or they did not. This is a huge benefit for using this grading system. It provides a great deal of information and does not punish, but informs the student about problems the student missed.

A template in the Appendix is available for grade organization.

ASSIGNING A GRADE VALUE TO STANDARD-BASED SCORING

O'Connor in *A Repair Kit for Grading: 15 Fixes for Broken Grades* (2007), shows teachers a method where grading is progressive. In this method, the student takes several formative assessments over the same content. This grading method relies on the idea that, as the students understanding progresses, their scores will rise as shown in Figure 30. The last formative assessment is then selected as the final and therefore summative assessment.

This method may work well in math or physical education where, students can be tested several times on the same content but may not work well in other content areas where there is less likely to be several summative assessments given for a single content target.

For example, in social studies, taking several unit assessments over the same content may not be practical. Typically, in many content areas, there may be several quizzes that only assess partial content understanding, formative assessments. Usually there is only one final assessment (summative) per unit.

With O'Connor's method (Figure 34), it is assumed that each formative assessment evaluates learning identical content. Therefore, the last formative assessment should show the greatest improvement. It is this last formative assessment that the teacher uses as a summative grade.

Figure 34

Formative Assessments Used as Summative Assessments

Adding Decimals Assessment	Adding Decimals Assessment	Adding Decimals Assessment	Adding Decimals Assessment	Final Assessment Score
1	2	2	3	3

As previously stated, the practicality of this approach to grading may be very low for many content areas. It is because many content areas primarily use a single summative assessment at the end of a unit grading this method is not practical. Even when allowing students to complete additional work to learn missing knowledge and then retesting.

It is helpful to consider that each assessment will have a total of 4 points, one for each level of the scoring rubric. Grade determination using the standard-based scoring method is statistically based more on a **modified mode** scale than a mean or averaging scale.

It is possible to create a standard-based grade without an electronic gradebook. In fact, sometimes this is easier for the teacher because there is great flexibility in creating a grade when not bound by the constraints of a software program.

Looking at a new grading scale can feel liberating and frightening at the same time. We will consider three different grading scales below: Flexible Standard-Based Grading Scale, Amended Flexible Standard-Based Grading Scale and the Electronic Gradebook Scale.

FLEXIBLE STANDARD BASED GRADING SCALE

> Looking at a new grading scale can feel liberating and the same time.

The Flexible Standard-Based Grading Scale is based on the mode of standard deviation. The mode score is the number that is repeated the most. Using the flexible grading method to assign a grade allows the teacher a great degree of flexibility about grade determination compared to the traditional system (see Figure 35).

Flexibility has sometimes been used synonymously with **subjectivity**.

If a student has more 3's than 2's or 1's, a student would receive a B grade. Similarly, the student who had more 4's than 3's, 2's or 1's then the student would receive an A grade.

Figure 35

Using a Flexible Standard-Based Grading Scale

Level 4: Mostly 4's = A
Level 3: Mostly 3's = B
Level 2: Mostly 2's = C
Level 1: Mostly 1's =D

Assuming the teacher does not have access to an electronic grading program, one advantage to this grading scale is there is no calculation. It takes very little time for the teacher to determine grades for student. A glance across a row of grades is enough to determine a grade.

Looking at Figure 36, when the student receives more 3's than any other score, the student would be awarded B grade. A disadvantage to the system can be seen below where the student receives a score of 1 for the World War 1 Assessment Summary. Teachers may feel that a student that receives a B should not also have accumulated such low scores as 1 or 0 in any summary assessments.

Figure 36

Example Standard- Based Gradebook

Level 1: Civil War Vocabulary Assessment	Level 2: Civil War Journal Assessment	Level 3: Civil War Target Assessment	Level 4: Civil War Advanced Assessment	**Civil War Assessment Summary**	Level 1: World War 1 Vocabulary Assessment	Level 2: World War 1 Journal Assessment	Level 3: World War 1 Target Assessment	Level 4: World War 1 Advanced Assessment	**World War 1 Assessment Summary**
1	1	1	0	3/4	1	0	0	0	1/4

Level 1: World War 2 Vocabulary Assessment	Level 2: World War 2 Journal Assessment	Level 3: World War 2 Target Assessment	Level 4: World War 2 Advanced Assessment	**World War 2 Assessment Summary**	Level 1: Korean War Vocabulary Assessment	Level 2: Korean War Journal Assessment	Level 3: Korean War Target Assessment	Level 4: Korean War Advanced Assessment	**Korean War Assessment Summary**
1	1	1	0	3/4	1	1	1	0	3/4

The score in the unit summary is the total points for levels 1 through 4 assessments. This summary allows students to see the complete picture of learning for each unit assessment. If one is using an electronic gradebook, the teacher can decide whether they want to publish all of the above information or just some of it. It has been the author's experience that the summary grade being a duplication of the previous four points is confusing to some parents and students.

Determining a grade in the above example, the scores in the summaries are as follows: 3, 3, 1, 3. According to the Flexible Standard-Based Grade Scale in Figure 32, the student would receive a B.

AMENDED FLEXIBLE STANDARD BASED GRADING SCALE

Additional conditions can be added to the grading scale if desired. If the teacher or team feels a student should not receive a B when the student has scored a 1 or 0 on a unit assessment summary then that can be built into grading criteria.

Figure 37

Amended Flexible Standard-Based Grading Scale

Level 4: Mostly 4's = A   No 0's or 1's
Level 3: Mostly 3's = B   No 0's or 1's
Level 2: Mostly 2's = C   No 0's
Level 1: Mostly 1's = D   No 0's

> Until a student proves they have done the necessary studying, there is no reason to give a second assessment when the outcome without studying is likely to be the same.

Now the student is restricted in the scores they may receive for each grade above (Figure 37). It is difficult to justify giving students higher scores like an A, B or C when they have zeros or ones.

Giving a student a second chance to improve a unit assessment is the author's preference only after a student has proven they have studied in advance. This can be done by assigning a set of problems that a student would complete about the concept or any other work appropriate which would teach students to learn the content upon work completion. For example, a student who fails a vocabulary assessment (level 1) may be required to write the words and the definitions 5 times each so show they have studied.

Until a student proves they have done the necessary studying, there is no reason to give a second assessment when the outcome without studying is likely to be the same. It also holds the student accountable for not having truly studied the first time the assessment was given.

ELECTRONIC GRADEBOOK SCALE

Using an electronic gradebook, while easier for the teacher also presents some challenges. The gradebook software requires the teacher to set percentage parameters for each grade: A, B, C, or D. These percentage parameters create more inflexibility in the grade determination. Percentages for each grade will be discussed in the next chapter.

Most grading programs have a grade override function where the teacher can change a grade of a student that has special circumstances (an IEP or has missed school due to a prolong illness).

When overriding a grade in an electronic gradebook, the teacher, of course, should document inside the program the justification for the grade change.

References:

Elder, Danelle, (2012): *Standard Based Teaching: A Classroom Guide.* http://www.amazon.com/Danelle-Elder-Standard-Based-Teaching/dp/B00N4FR7R2

O'Connor, K. (2007). *A Repair Kit for Grading: 15 Fixes for Broken Grades*, ETS/ATI. Portland, OR

CHAPTER 8:

DETERMINING THE GRADING SCALE PERCENTAGE FOR GRADE ASSIGNMENT

Grading scale percentages can be determined by an individual teacher, department, school or district. Of course when groups of teachers determine the percentage for the grading scale the agreement process may be lengthy. Everyone must come to the same understanding and decision about a grading scale.

To help the process of determining a grading scale, looking at the scenarios below will help the teacher to mentally frame parameters. Also, it may be helpful to use the **template** provided in the Appendix in a professional development setting so everyone has opportunity to discuss their beliefs and ideas.

It is simple to say that a student will receive a C grade when they mostly score twos. However, teachers may want a percentage to follow as a guideline for grade determination.

In Figure 38, example scores are given so the percentage score may be determined.

Figure 38

Using Scoring Trends for Grade Determination

	Assessment 1	Assessment 2	Assessment 3	Assessment 4	Assessment 5	Assessment 6
Student 1	3	3	3	3	3	3
Student 2	2	3	3	3	3	3
Student 3	2	2	3	3	3	3
Student 4	2	2	2	3	3	3
Student 5	2	2	2	2	3	3

Start by considering the score the student should receive if they are going to make a B grade or a C grade. In Figure 38, one can see a simplified version of the grade book where students receive scores of 3's and 2's.

In Figure 39, the student scores have been totaled. The average scores range from 3.0 to 2.33. The percentage for the scores is calculated out a four-point scale because each assessment has four levels. Thus percentage must be considered from a base of four points.

Figure 39

Comparing Trends to Percentages

Student Names	Totaled Scores	Average of Scores	Percentage of Scores Using a 4 point scale
Student 1	18	3.0	75%
Student 2	17	2.83	71%
Student 3	16	2.66	66%
Student 4	15	2.5	63%
Student 5	14	2.33	58%

It is important not to fall into the trap of using the old traditional mean system of grading when examining the percentage.

Because these scores are scaffold scores, they do not follow the same pattern as the traditional grading system. What is necessary to think about when constructing grade cutoffs for the first time, is to look at miscellaneous student scores, Figure 39, and determine what is an acceptable value for an A grade, B grade, C grade, and D grade. This is important to the foundation of standard-based grading when considering percentage construction for grade assignment.

Figure 40

Pie Chart with Rubric Content Breakdown

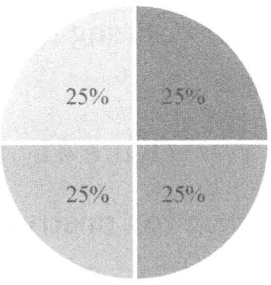

- Level 1 Content Assessment
- Level 2 Content Assessment
- Level 3 Content Assessment
- Level 4 Content Assessment

In Figure 40, each level grade to 25% of learning. The mathematical breakdown for this is as follows:

Level 1: 25% of learning

Level 2: 25% of learning

Level 3: 25% of learning

Level 4: 25% of learning

Because each level supports only 25% of learning, there is no chunk of learning larger than any other in the traditional mean system of grading.

The grading scale is designed to determine a grade from an accumulation of scoring rubrics, (level 1, level 2, etc.). It may be easier to start conceptualizing the proper scale construction by looking at Figure 41.

Figure 41

A Scale Breakdown to Construct Grade Percentage

Percentage Scale	Example Assessment Scores	4 Point Scale Equivalent	Grade Equivalent
100 %	4 4 4 4	4.0	A
94 %	4 4 4 3	3.75	A
88 %	4 4 3 3	3.5	A-
81 %	4 3 3 3	3.25	B+
75 %	3 3 3 3	3.0	B
69 %	3 3 3 2	2.75	B
63 %	3 3 2 2	2.5	B-
56 %	3 2 2 2	2.25	C+
50 %	2 2 2 2	2.0	C
44 %	2 2 2 1	1.75	C
38 %	2 2 1 1	1.5	C-
31 %	2 1 1 1	1.25	D+
25 %	1 1 1 1	1.0	D

The above figure is merely an example to help the teacher begin the thinking process, linking the percentage scale to the point scale through assessment scores.

A template is provided for professional development purposes which will help facilitate discussion with staff about the value of an A, B, C and D grade (Figure 42).

Figure 42

Professional Development Using a Grading Scales Template

Letter Value	Description of level difficulty	Scoring examples acceptable for this level	Percentages that reflect example scoring
* A	Regularly achieved **advanced** understanding		
A-			
B+			
* B	Regularly achieved target **mastery**		
B-			
C+			
* C	Regularly achieved **partial** or most **basic** understanding of target		
C-			
* D+			
* D	Very little understanding of target		

In this template, * has been marked as priority decisions. These letter values must be discussed first. All other decisions should be based on their values where the target score is a B. Start by determining what a B letter grade means. Then determine the other letters with an A being the last letter value determined.

The above template can be used by departments and staff as a beginning point when processing grade values. The staff should simply plug in assessment scores and then talk about whether they can support those values for each grade.

Caution: This process normally takes time and care if done properly. Teachers need to be given ample time to process and develop new grading percentages for each grade. To rush this process only creates anxiety and a disbelief in the standard-based system.

> This process normally takes time and care if done properly.

It is important to **avoid language** about the excellence, average or failure of individual grades. **These are judgments and have no place when communicating to students their academic achievement.**

Further, there is no reason why anyone would need to create a value for an A+. The concept of an A representing advanced understanding is as high as understanding can be measured. Anything above that scale only promotes graded inflation (Slavov, 2013) which has become a real problem in colleges and universities across the nation. Slavov reports:

> A recent study of 200 colleges and universities found that more than 40 percent of all grades awarded were in the A range. Some have argued that these inflated grades are necessary to help students get ahead in a competitive job market. While that might be true for an individual professor or university, at the national level, grade inflation is a negative-sum game that imposes serious costs on society.

With the increase in the use of A+, along with other factors, high school GPAs are increasing but SAT scores are not matching these increases (Bracey, 1994).

Bracey has already confirmed grade inflation is occurring in high schools. The trend continues in colleges and universities across America as seen in the graph below, Figure 43. This graph is from the Teacher College Report Article (2012). It clearly shows the percentages of A's rising while the percentages of B's and C's are falling.

It is interesting to note that the percentage of F's has remained the same for nearly 70 years.

Figure 43

Grade Distribution Over Time, Nationwide

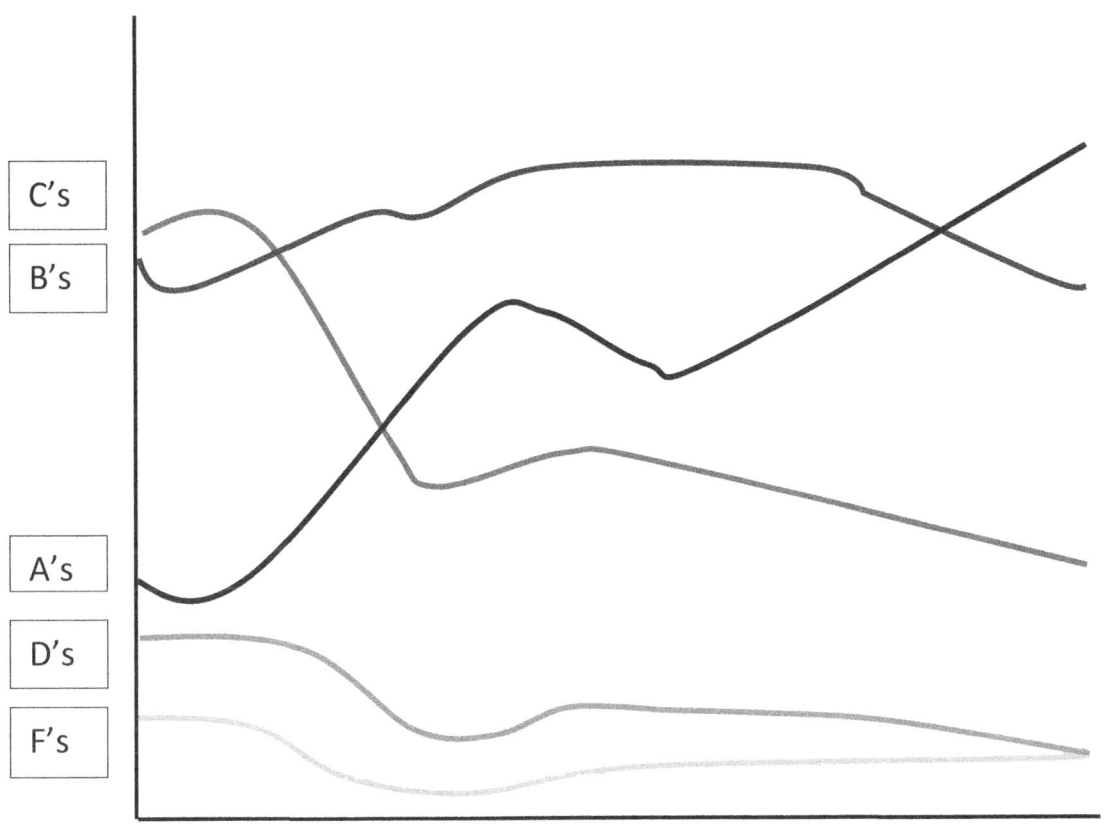

Grade Distribution From 1940-2008

When considering grading percentage scale, teachers, parents and schools need to participate in a serious and open dialogue about rigor and fairness of the grading. This dialogue must include teachers, administrators and even parents.

To conclude, below in Figure 44, is an example of what a gradebook can look like using the standard-based grading system.

Figure 44

Electronic Gradebook Example

Student	Grade	Level 1 Water Cycle	Level 2 Water Cycle	Level 3 Water Cycle	Level 4 Water Cycle	Journal Water Cycle
Tom		1	1	1	1	0
Joan		1	1	1	1	4
Harry		0	0	0	0	2
Ali		1	1	0	0	2

(An actual copy of an electronic gradebook could not be used because of photo quality issues.)

Each learning level is identified and separated. **Discussions with students center exclusively on which level the student passed and where the student needs more study.**

In the example above, the exception to single point scoring is the Water Cycle Journal Assessment where all four points were awarded at one time when journals were evaluated. More on journaling using a standard-based system can be found in Standard-Based Journaling: A Classroom Guide (Elder, 2015).

This particular electronic gradebook is limited as to what grade a teacher may enter. There is no Incomplete or (I) in this electronic program. The only option was a zero to show the student did not pass an assessment level.

Incomplete is preferable when students do not complete assignments. An incomplete grade can be set to calculate as a zero or ignored if the teacher desires. However, using an (I) instead of an (F) sends a different message to students, parent and teachers. The message is the student has not shown enough evidence of learning to achieve any other score.

> We need to focus student accomplishments.

We need to focus on student accomplishments, allowing our conversations and grades to focus on the mastery of learning, not the judgment associated with failure or being average.

Reference:

Bracey, G. W. (1994). Bracey Report, Phi Delta Kappan, 76, 115-127

Slavov, Sita, (2013). US News Week, How to Fix College Grade Inflation, From Traditional grading to Standard Based Grading, Dec. 26, 2013

Rojstaczer, Stuart & Healy, Christopher, (2012). *Where A Is Ordinary: The Evolution of American College and University Grading, 1940–2009*, Teachers College Record, http://www.gradeinflation.com/tcr2011grading.pdf

CHAPTER 9:

WHAT HOLDS TEACHERS BACK FROM ACCEPTING THE STANDARD-BASED TEACHING MODEL?

What keeps teachers from changing to the standard- based grading system?

> Part of what keeps a teacher from changing grading systems is cultural.

A teacher's grading system is like the Holy Grail of teaching. Even legislators can't tell teachers how to grade. Though, if they had the power, they surely would.

Part of what keeps a teacher from changing grading systems is cultural. All teachers have grown up in nearly the same grading environment. They are the products of the traditional mean system of grading. This creates a cultural loyalty to this system.

Part of what keeps a teacher from changing grading systems is the fear of the unknown. So much pressure has been heaped upon teachers, it is inconceivable that teachers, themselves, with willingly create unnecessary pressure to change to system that they are unfamiliar with.

Part of what keeps a teacher from changing grading systems is a paucity of proper professional development. Districts need to provide deep support when asking teachers to change their grading system. Providing a small, introductory professional development exposure will only create confusion when a teacher is expected that to completely shift to a standard-based grading system. In this scenario, the teacher will default to the traditional mean system of grading, a known commodity.

Buildings and districts need to develop educational communities where teachers can ask questions and problems, solutions to roadblocks.

Forcing teachers to change without a support system and ongoing professional development, leaves them resentful without proper processing and input opportunities. Dictating the use of a grading system where teachers have no opportunity to ask questions does not promote schema change. Expecting teachers to accept system without professional support and time ask questions (and sometimes vent) is a mistake. This policy will likely not lead to long-term change and acceptance.

> Part of what keeps a teacher from changing grading systems is lack of time to learn the grading and scoring process.

Part of what keeps a teacher from changing grading systems is the unwillingness by districts to allow experimentation. Using the standard-based grading system mentioned in this series takes some trial and error to perfect. Principals and districts cannot expect a teacher to simply convert and immediately become expert in the new system.

Part of what keeps a teacher from changing grading systems is lack of time to learn the grading and scoring process. When changing to a new grading system, there needs to be time for educational growth. This reinforcement needs to be a priority by principals and districts so teachers can grow in their understanding without evaluation pressures.

Finally, part of what keeps a teacher from changing grading systems is the perception that a standard-based grading system does not address behavior. Behavior needs to be addressed separately and not included in the academic grade.

It is the author hopes that this series, the **Standard-Based Classroom Guide Series** will eliminate some of these barriers.

BEHAVIOR VS. ACADEMIC REPORTING

Grading and reporting should be restricted to standard evaluation goals only.

This means, for example, that a student cannot be docked points on an assignment that is handed in late. Late assignment denote a behavior problem. Only academic assessments of content or process/procedure being evaluated create scores for grading purposes.

> Homework is simply a formative check for understanding.

What is a teacher to do when a student constantly turns homework late? Homework is simply a formative check on understanding. Homework can be done by anyone at home and so therefore cannot be considered evidence of learning.

When a student turns work in late, it is a behavior problem. Reducing an academic evaluation of student knowledge because of a behavior blurs the success the score reports about the students understanding of knowledge. When the student receives a score that is reduced because the student's work is late, the changed score, in essence, reduces the proof about the student's achievement.

Problem behavior examples are:

- late work
- off-task behavior
- tardy to class
- not bringing materials to class
- disruptive in class
- disrespectful
- incomplete work
- problems following directions.

> Teachers need to be able to address behavior.

Behavior information should not be represented in the scoring rubric and so cannot be part of a grade. However, teachers need to be able to address and report behavior. It is also important for parents to be informed and acknowledge student misbehavior. Behavior information must be reported so parents can fully understand why students are not being academically successful.

BEHAVIOR REPORTING

There are a couple methods teachers can report about student behavior.

1) A separate report can be created for students and parents to receive information about student behavior problems;
2) Regular behavior reporting in an electronic gradebook.

Creating a separate report for parents is very useful if the grade report allows for such reporting. If the grade card does not allow for the reporting of behavior, the teacher can construct their own.

Constructing one's own report for behavior is of little consequence if there is no opportunity for parents to see it. These reports can be given at student-led conferences or separately mailed home, if money and time allow.

It is important to remember that a behavior rubric is not a scoring rubric. **It is a quality measurement.** Therefore, creating a rubric for behavior is different than creating a scoring rubric.

It is important that there be several divisions in this rubric so the content is broken up appropriately for scaffolding. The scoring rubric is based on the four levels. Each level progresses in complexity regarding the standard being taught.

A behavior rubric should not be 'chunked' in the same way. A behavior rubric is not a dichotomous decision. There needs to be a 'gray area' in this decision. It is not black or white...point or no point determination. An added step is required where a student shows behavior is not at an optimum but it's not completely unacceptable. This step is necessary to show growth.

When viewing behavior rubrics from websites, a plethora of examples are available. Many examples, such as in Figure 41, divided behavior in the four levels as though they are the scoring rubric. This creates an **enormous** 'gray' zone where it is not necessary for the student's behavior to change.

Looking at time management in the example below, Figure 45, there really is no difference between levels one and two for student behavior. *The student rarely manages time while* versus *the student manages time poorly* are really the same statement. Neither behavior is acceptable.

Behavior Rubric and Report Card

Figure 45

Behaviors	4	3	2	1
Time Management	The student is on task most of the time	The student is on task some of the time	The student is rarely on task	The student is never on task
Materials in Class	The student has materials most of the time	The student has materials some of the time	The student rarely has materials in class	The student never has materials in class

> Using statements like 'rarely' and 'never' are ineffective when trying to improve. .behavior

Using statements like 'rarely' and 'never' are ineffective when trying to improve behavior. A student who rarely brings materials to class nor uses time well is hardly different than a student that never does. The distinction wastes time and energy, giving no new information about student behavior.

What then is the most useful way to evaluate a student's behavior?

There is really only three points necessary when communicating student behavior in the classroom.

1) The student is achieving the behavior desired by the teacher.
2) The student sometimes is achieving the desired behavior.
3) The student's behavior is unacceptable.

The teacher needs to send a clear message to the student about his/her behavior. The best way is to be open honest and when communicating about student behavior. Either the student is performing appropriately or they are not. If they are not performing appropriately, can some credit be given or not?

Having a three point behavior rubric reveals the student's behavior when appropriate, sometimes appropriate (gray zone) or inappropriate (Figure 46).

In this report, the teacher can add which behaviors the student needs to improve under the three behavior boxes in Figure 46. Be sure to focus on the most important behaviors that needs changing. Adding more than three or four may be too many for the student to concentrate on.

These reports are usually made daily in the classroom with parents receiving them that day from the student or email. A weekly report to parents may be enough to keep the parent advised. This report can also be part of an electronic report that parents can view regularly.

This report can be used as a daily check for students if behavior warrants it or whenever the teacher needs help reinforcing proper behavior in the classroom.

Behavior Report Card Using Numbers

Figure 46

Subject/Class	Behavior:	Behavior:	Behavior:	Behavior:
	2 1 0 Comment:	2 1 0 Comment:	2 1 0 Comment:	2 1 0 Comment:
	2 1 0 Comment:	2 1 0 Comment:	2 1 0 Comment:	2 1 0 Comment:
	2 1 0 Comment:	2 1 0 Comment:	2 1 0 Comment:	2 1 0 Comment:

2= appropriate, 1= sometimes appropriate, 0= inappropriate

> It is important that the points students received for poor behavior are not associated with grade performance.

This method allows opportunity to show growth and at the same time clearly signals to students there are behavior thresholds that must be reached to earn the mark for appropriate behavior.

It is important that the points students received for poor behavior are not associated with grade performance.

Teachers and administrators may be tempted to total the scores in this report. This creates blurriness about the student behavior. **Inappropriate behaviors must be separated and targeted**

separately so each behavior improvement can be addressed. Each behavior improvement, then can be celebrated on its own when appropriate. To create a total maybe useful for graphing purposes to look at overall growth but it may not something the student would see daily.

To avoid the confusion of behavior vs academic points, symbols may better represent levels of behavior. In Figure 47, faces are used to represent behavior levels. These represent emotions associated with the behaviors of the student.

Behavior Report Card Using Faces

Figure 47

Subject/ Class	Behavior:	Behavior:	Behavior:	Behavior:
	☺ ☺ ☹ Comments:	☺ ☺ ☹ Comments:	☺ ☺ ☹ Comments:	☺ ☺ ☹ Comments:
	☺ ☺ ☹ Comments:	☺ ☺ ☹ Comments:	☺ ☺ ☹ Comments:	☺ ☺ ☹ Comments:
	☺ ☺ ☹ Comments:	☺ ☺ ☹ Comments:	☺ ☺ ☹ Comments:	☺ ☺ ☹ Comments:

☺= appropriate, ☺= sometimes appropriate, ☹= inappropriate

Any symbol can represent behavior in a behavior report. Below in Figure 48, letters represent behavior performance.

Behavior Report Card Using Letters

Figure 48

Subject/Class	Behavior:	Behavior:	Behavior:	Behavior:
	A S I Comments:	A S I Comments:	A S I Comments:	A S I Comments:
	A S I Comments:	A S I Comments:	A S I Comments:	A S I Comments:
	A S I Comments:	A S I Comments:	A S I Comments:	A S I Comments:

> Teachers must be consistent as possible when evaluating student performance!

A= appropriate, S= sometimes appropriate, I= inappropriate

In figure 44, the same card is used with letters to represent behaviors. The letters represent A= Appropriate, S= Sometimes Appropriate and I = Inappropriate.

These three behavior cards can be found in the template appendix.

TEACHER CONSISTENCY

Teachers must be as consistent as possible when evaluating student performance! Jim Wright, Intervention Specialist in

Syracuse, New York, sites teacher inconsistency as one of the most difficult elements to address when gauging the success of a behavior report.

Wright says it is important to define the behavior **clearly** and that the student is to be accountable. Thus, the teacher must communicate clearly about behavior and score the behavior consistently.

It may be helpful then, where several teachers are evaluating the same student's behavior, for those teachers to agree to the same behavior descriptors.

Further, he states that graphing the student behavior over time helps show the student and all stake holders the progress of the student.

> **Do not give students the highest behavior mark unless the student behavior is truly appropriate.**

One last note: Do not give students the highest behavior mark unless the student behavior is truly appropriate. The point of this report is to clearly communicate to the student (and other interested parties) the difference between appropriate and inappropriate behavior.

Administrators, other teachers and parents may use this report to determine the future placement or program eligibility of the student when reviewing the behavior report.

Feeling sorry for a student and then inflating his/her behavior score only sabotages the efforts of all involved. Most importantly it sends a message to the student that he/she does not need to change inappropriate behaviors.

Here is the bottom line... students need to manage their own behavior. An employer will fire a destructive employee. College professors will not pass a destructive student. A student must come to terms with what he/she wants to succeed in these areas and, if so, is genuinely willing to adjust his/her behavior.

Reference:

Wright, Jim (2003). Classroom Behavior Report Card Resource Book, http://www.jimwrightonline.com/pdfdocs/tbrc/tbrcmanual.pdf

THE LAST WORD

About the templates...

Templates are forms that should change when you need them to be different. The templates in this book are just a stepping off point. No author can presume that their contributions to the educational society is beyond revision by the expert in the classroom... the teacher. You may want to change the templates in this appendix or you may grow out of their use altogether.

About publishing...

I really want to encourage teachers and principals to publish their ideas. Publish what you know works in schools and classrooms. Teachers and principals need to be seen in America as experts in their own field. They need to be given the respect their expertise requires. Until this happens, I feel the powers in education will only continue to look outside schools for the answers to problems in our current educational system.

Teachers must be seen as solution creators. No one knows more than they about the classroom and how it functions.

TEMPLATE APPENDIX

Revised Blooms Taxonomy by Anderson and Krathwohl's Taxonomy 2001

1. **Remembering:** Recognizing or recalling knowledge from memory by using definitions, facts, or lists, or recitation as evidence of learning.

2. **Understanding:** Demonstrating meaning by preforming interpretation, classification, summarization, inferring, comparing, graphing and explaining as evidence of learning.

3. **Applying:** Execution of a procedure. Applying knowledge to situations of learned material by using models, reports, sketches, presentations, interviews or diagramming as evidence of learning.

4. **Analyzing:** Dividing a concept into pieces, determining how these pieces relate to one another through differentiation, organization or comparing by using spreadsheets, surveys, charts, diagrams or graphic representations as evidence of learning.

5. **Evaluating:** Making judgments based on criteria and standards through checking and critiquing by using recommendations, testing or defending conclusions as evidence of learning.

6. **Creating:** Designing or putting elements together to form a functional or working whole to create a new pattern or structure through generating, planning or inventing as evidence of learning.

Taxonomy Selection Template

Revised Blooms Taxonomy Level	Verb Associated With Revised Blooms Level	Chosen Rubric Level Associated With Verb	Rubric Level Description
Creating			
Evaluating			
Analyzing			
Applying			
Understanding			
Remembering			

Note: There are only four levels in a rubric, therefore only four taxonomy levels can be used as evidence of learning. The teacher must decide which taxonomy level best reflects the desired standard action then build the rest of the rubric around that action.

Rubric Construction Template

Topic:
Unit Concept:
State Standard Classification:
Target:
Rubric Title:

Incomplete Evidence of Learning (Incomplete)	Level 1: Foundation for Target	Level 2: Simple Bridge Concept	Level 3: Target Proficiency	Level 4: Advanced Application of Target
	I can…	I can…	I can…	I can…

D. Elder ☒ 2015

Professional Development Using a Grading Scales Template

Letter Value	Description of level difficulty	Scoring examples acceptable for this level	Percentages that reflect example scoring
* A	Regularly achieved **advanced** understanding		
A-			
B+			
* B	Regularly achieved target **mastery**		
B-			
C+			
* C	Regularly achieved **partial** or most **basic** understanding of target		
C-			
* D+			
* D	Very little understanding of target		

In this template, * has been marked as priority decisions. These letter values must be discussed first. All other decisions should be based on their values where the target score is a B. Start by determining what a B letter grade means. Then determine the other letters with an A being the last letter value determined.

Unit Alignment Guide

◊ Students have a Table of Contents which has a column to mark levels.

◊ At the very beginning of a unit, students are given a scoring rubric with each level description.

◊ Students set goals for mastering each level.

◊ Students are given time to use appropriate strategies to study each level.

◊ Students a given simple exit tasks where they evaluate their understanding of a particular level.

◊ Students are given a study guide that has a sample problem for each level.

◊ Students are given an assessment where each level is separate and scored separately.

◊ Students evaluate their success at learning each level.

◊ The teacher enters a **differentiated score** for each level (a separate score which can later be summarized).

◊ The teacher provides a relearning and retesting experience for students on assessment levels that where not mastered when evidence of studying has been presented to the teacher.

Behavior Report Card Using Numbers

Subject/Class	Behavior:	Behavior:	Behavior:	Behavior:
	2 1 0 Comment:	2 1 0 Comment:	2 1 0 Comment:	2 1 0 Comment:
	2 1 0 Comment:	2 1 0 Comment:	2 1 0 Comment:	2 1 0 Comment:
	2 1 0 Comment:	2 1 0 Comment:	2 1 0 Comment:	2 1 0 Comment:
	2 1 0 Comment:	2 1 0 Comment:	2 1 0 Comment:	2 1 0 Comment:
	2 1 0 Comment:	2 1 0 Comment:	2 1 0 Comment:	2 1 0 Comment:
	2 1 0 Comment:	2 1 0 Comment:	2 1 0 Comment:	2 1 0 Comment:

2= Appropriate Behavior

1= Sometimes Appropriate Behavior

0= Inappropriate Behavior

Behavior Report Card Using Faces

Subject/ Class	Behavior:	Behavior:	Behavior:	Behavior:
	☺ ☻ ☹ Comments:	☺ ☻ ☹ Comments:	☺ ☻ ☹ Comments:	☺ ☻ ☹ Comments:
	☺ ☻ ☹ Comments:	☺ ☻ ☹ Comments:	☺ ☻ ☹ Comments:	☺ ☻ ☹ Comments:
	☺ ☻ ☹ Comments:	☺ ☻ ☹ Comments:	☺ ☻ ☹ Comments:	☺ ☻ ☹ Comments:
	☺ ☻ ☹ Comments:	☺ ☻ ☹ Comments:	☺ ☻ ☹ Comments:	☺ ☻ ☹ Comments:
	☺ ☻ ☹ Comments:	☺ ☻ ☹ Comments:	☺ ☻ ☹ Comments:	☺ ☻ ☹ Comments:
	☺ ☻ ☹ Comments:	☺ ☻ ☹ Comments:	☺ ☻ ☹ Comments:	☺ ☻ ☹ Comments:

☺ = Appropriate Behavior

☻ = Sometimes Appropriate Behavior

☹ = Inappropriate Behavior

Behavior Report Card Using Letters

Subject/Class	Behavior:	Behavior:	Behavior:	Behavior:
	A S I Comments:	A S I Comments:	A S I Comments:	A S I Comments:
	A S I Comments:	A S I Comments:	A S I Comments:	A S I Comments:
	A S I Comments:	A S I Comments:	A S I Comments:	A S I Comments:
	A S I Comments:	A S I Comments:	A S I Comments:	A S I Comments:
	A S I Comments:	A S I Comments:	A S I Comments:	A S I Comments:
	A S I Comments:	A S I Comments:	A S I Comments:	A S I Comments:

A = Appropriate Behavior

S = Sometimes Appropriate Behavior

I = Inappropriate Behavior

Made in United States
Orlando, FL
03 October 2023